Unleashing the Power of PR

Mark Weiner

Unleashing the Power of PR

A Contrarian's Guide to Marketing and Communication

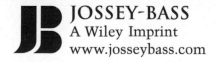

IABC INTERNATIONAL ASSOCIATION OF BUSINESS COMMUNICATORS

JB JOSSEY-BASS
A Wiley Imprint
www.josseybass.com

Published by Jossey-Bass
A Wiley Imprint
989 Market Street, San Francisco, CA 94103-1741   www.josseybass.com

Jossey-Bass books and products are available through most bookstores. To contact Jossey-Bass directly call our Customer Care Department within the U.S. at 800-956-7739, outside the U.S. at 317-572-3986, or fax 317-572-4002.

Jossey-Bass also publishes its books in a variety of electronic formats. Some content that appears in print may not be available in electronic books.

Library of Congress Cataloging-in-Publication Data

Weiner, Mark, 1946–
 Unleashing the power of PR : a contrarian's guide to marketing and communication / Mark Weiner.
      p. cm.
 "A joint publication of the Jossey-Bass business & management series and the International Association of Business Communicators."
 Includes index.
 ISBN-13: 978-0-7879-8279-9 (cloth)
 ISBN-10: 0-7879-8279-2 (cloth)
 1. Public relations. 2. Business communication. 3. Communication in marketing. I. International Association of Business Communicators.
II. Title. III. Series: Jossey-Bass business & management series.
 HD59.W37 2006
 659.2—dc22

                                                            2006008660

Printed in the United States of America
FIRST EDITION
HB Printing   10 9 8 7 6 5 4 3 2 1

A Joint Publication of

The Jossey-Bass

Business & Management Series

and

The International Association

of Business Communicators

Contents

Appendixes

Foreword

The book you are holding in your hands was written by a self-professed contrarian. According to my dictionary, a *contrarian* is "one who takes a contrary view or action and makes decisions that contradict prevailing wisdom." That's a bold stance. Mark Weiner and I first discussed the idea for this book when we met in Belgium in 2004. He offered a compelling and passionate argument about dispelling myths and breaking away from the conventional thinking that communication, and PR as a subset of communication, can't be measured, is too expensive, and is not well understood. As with many projects, the book went in a number of directions before taking the path outlined in these pages. But the original intent remained the same, to provide a framework for defining what had been intangible and proving and improving the return on investment of PR within the broader context of marketing communication.

The fact that good communication is important in any organization is obvious. Yet the intangible nature of communication makes its effectiveness incredibly difficult to prove. Consider the difference between an organization that offers its customers a clear picture of its services and one that does not—one that maps out and communicates its strategic direction for its employees and one that does not. Good reputation hinges not only on a company's ability to produce a quality product but also on its ability to clearly communicate with every stakeholder at each step of the life of that product. Although we know this is true, determining how to outline these facts in a way that makes sense to the powers that be has been a long and difficult journey.

Organizational communication's return on investment has been a crucial question for the business communication profession since it emerged three decades ago, and was among the most critical issues for IABC (the International Association of Business Communicators) when it formed in 1970. In 1991 the IABC Research Foundation published its first book from the landmark "Excellence" study, offering some of the first evidence of a linkage between excellent communication and organizational success. The study began in 1984 and was conducted by James and Larissa Grunig from the University of Maryland, along with David Dozier of San Diego State University. It sought to identify the characteristics of an excellent communication department and answer the questions, "How does public relations contribute to organizational effectiveness?" and "What is that contribution worth?"

The researchers found that even organizations with excellent public relations had a hard time attaching a monetary value to their communication. Still, the researchers made some key discoveries, including the identification of eight basic principles that made public relations most effective: managing strategically, having a senior communicator report to senior management, and having a department that encompasses all communication functions, stresses two-way interaction with strategic publics, has a symmetrical approach to public relations, and strives to create win-win solutions to common problems or issues. An excellent communication department places the senior communication practitioner with critical knowledge in a managerial role, creates equal opportunities for its employees, uses activism as a way to move the organization forward, has support from top management, and operates within the framework of a supportive organizational culture.

Just as the "Excellence" study answered questions, it also raised many, spawning more books associated with the study as well as additional studies from the IABC Research Foundation. These studies provided the basis for articles, conference sessions, seminars, and books that tackled the issue of how to measure and evaluate the communication function in a way that linked it to the strategic objectives of the organization, especially its effect on the bottom line. It's interesting that more than twenty years later, this topic is still at the top of the agenda for most communication professionals. The perennial question of communication's return on investment continues to hold our attention, and new visionaries have taken on the challenge of addressing that question. How do you take something that you *know* is important and prove it in a way that is compelling to the leaders of the organization?

As communication professionals have evolved from tacticians to strategists, measurement has grown from a series of random ideas and steps to a science that has a clear direction and real-world application. With each year since the development of studies like the "Excellence" project, new experts have developed ways to identify desired outcomes, employ proper measurement techniques, and apply their limited resources with the biggest impact. In this book, Mark Weiner applies his years of experience with Delahaye to offer case studies and analyses that break down the science of PR measurement in a way that is easy to understand and apply. The book offers a fresh and innovative approach that takes the profession one step closer to understanding and demonstrating the value of organizational communication. On behalf of IABC, I'd like to thank Mark Weiner for contributing to the communication profession by sharing his knowledge of public relations and lending his time and expertise, and for his unending patience and commitment to this project.

NATASHA SPRING
Executive Editor, *Communication World*
Vice President, Publishing and Research
International Association of
Business Communicators (IABC)

Preface

Public relations and corporate communications are at a crossroads. New communication technologies and methodologies such as the Internet, blogs, cable and satellite TV providers that deliver more than five hundred channels, and TiVo are changing the competitive landscape—and increasingly casting doubt on the effectiveness of mass-market advertising and promotion strategies. Moreover, a strict business imperative that demands a demonstrable return on investment is forcing corporate and marketing communication decision makers to think in new ways. For their part, marketers are turning away from money-losing promotions and coupon marketing, which have failed on the promise to build brand loyalty. Today's tumultuous environment is creating new opportunities for and new threats to corporate communications.

Public relations (PR), the traditional underdog of the marketing mix, has the most to gain in this new business atmosphere. In fact, PR can supplant paid media in many ways, upset traditional marketing philosophies, and do much to provide what advertisers and direct marketers desperately pursue: customer involvement, message credibility, and brand value. New applications of public relations research and advanced statistical analyses clearly demonstrate PR's ability to drive sales and to deliver a strong return on investment (ROI) in terms of lowering overall communication and marketing costs while at the same time delivering meaningful business outcomes in terms of sales and other measurable results. PR has also been shown to accelerate other forms of corporate and marketing communication by making them even more effective. Yet, until now, few PR professionals have been able to take advantage of this research.

Unleashing the Power of PR takes you inside the world of PR research and shows you how it can be used to strengthen PR programs of all sorts. Based on my twenty years of experience in quantitative and qualitative research and evaluation techniques for scores of the world's leading organizations, this book explains how to use market research methods to plan and evaluate public relations programs scientifically. I go beyond theory and—using dozens of case studies—show the powerful role that research can play in crafting public relations programs that generate demonstrable business outcomes. Along the way, I explode dozens of myths about PR—held by PR practitioners *and* the executives to whom they report—myths that undercut the effectiveness of PR and obscure its real value.

Measuring the Power of PR

One of the great myths in the field of public relations is that PR, driven as it is by relationships and creativity, is impossible to measure. To the contrary, public relations in today's business environment is as much science as it is art—and its contribution can be quantified. As marketers continue to gain more control over marketing intelligence as a way to better understand market conditions, information is emerging on the relative abilities of the whole range of agents in the marketing mix—including PR—to drive sales. And the truth is that PR is more powerful than generally realized: this book demonstrates and documents how public relations can be used as a low-cost, high-value alternative for achieving meaningful business outcomes.

My firm has been involved with dozens of these marketing mix analyses—and in every case, public relations delivers among the very best values, at par with advertising and frequently much better than advertising, promotions, coupons, special events, and all the rest. To take a real-life example, a study Delahaye did for a beer company showed that one dollar invested in mass-market television advertising yielded about $1.10 in sales, whereas one dollar spent on PR yielded $8.00 in sales. In dozens of categories from telecom to automotive and from financial services to consumer packaged goods, our research confirms that the relative yield of public relations is as good as—and more often better than—that of any other form of marketing. Needless to say, the implications for PR spending are enormous: a shift of only a few percentage points of TV advertising dollars into the average public relations program would effectively double or even triple the average PR budget.

So why don't PR professionals and marketing executives use the available research tools to assess and strengthen PR programs? In talking to senior executives and PR people, I have found that the executives don't know enough about PR to ask for the proper measures, and the hands-on practitioners don't know enough about what's available in the field of PR research to apply to the programs over which they are responsible. For example, PR professionals generally fall back on "volume of press clippings" when asked for a key measure of PR effectiveness. Yet numerous surveys show that the executives to whom PR people report consider "volume of press clippings" the least important measure of effectiveness. It doesn't have to be this way. PR professionals and business executives do not have to talk past each other. They can learn to speak a common language based on measurable business results. One central purpose of this book is to build that language and show how doing so can strengthen PR performance and results.

Dozens of rigorous surveys among thousands of PR's internal clients at large organizations around the world have helped uncover the value systems decision makers use in assessing PR performance and planning PR programs. Routinely, these surveys reveal that these decision makers favor measures that are *reasonable, meaningful,* and *measurable;* "delivering key messages to target audiences" and "raising awareness" top the list. This book will show you how to come up with reasonable, meaningful, and measurable criteria that you can use to demonstrate the value of your PR efforts to decision makers.

While demonstrating value is important, improving the ROI of your PR efforts is critical. And here again, scientific research tools can be used to strengthen public relations. This book shows how research can be used in planning to shape PR strategy and fine-tune PR tactics, as well as how research can be used to evaluate the results of PR campaigns to make mid-course corrections and inform future campaigns.

A Look Ahead

In Part One, two chapters detail the opportunities presented and the challenges posed by the emerging realities shaping marketing and corporate communications. Chapter One outlines seven elements of change—including transformations in the media business, the decline of traditional mass marketing, and decreasing brand loyalty—that have altered the environment of corporate and marketing communications; it shows how these new conditions offer new opportunities for PR as a cost-effective means for achieving real business results. In Chapter Two I explain how new demands for accountability and measurable results are increasing the pressure on PR departments and agencies and how conventional marketing wisdom often undermines PR efforts to meet these challenges. In addition, I outline the eleven critical questions you must ask before launching a PR program and discuss ways formal and informal research tools can be used to answer them.

The four chapters of Part Two explain the core elements of a scientific approach to public relations in detail. Chapter Three shows how a disciplined, research-based approach to public relations and corporate communication can clarify what works and what doesn't so that weak programs can be turned around or eliminated and successful ones can be reinforced. I discuss a variety of research tools including Journalist Audits, Executive Audits, media content analysis, and marketing mix modeling.

In Chapter Four I explain why setting clear, measurable objectives is so important at the outset of any public relations program; show how to use research in the process of setting objectives; describe how to set reasonable, meaningful, and measurable objectives; and detail how to obtain top management buy-in for the objectives you develop. Once your public relations objectives are established, the task becomes to shape your strategy and tactics to achieve those objectives, the subject of the next chapter.

Chapter Five clears up the confusion that often envelops thinking about tactics and strategy and how they differ, explains the role of research in shaping an effective public relations strategy, offers suggestions for avoiding pitfalls in the strategy development process, and describes how to select and shape tactics that are appropriate for your strategy.

Chapter Six explains why evaluation is not simply a postmortem exercise but an ongoing process and a means for managing continual improvement in public relations. I explain that using research-based evaluation can tell you more than just *what happened*, it can also tell you *why it happened, if it will continue*, and *what should be done about it*.

Part Three shows how you can put research-based tools to work in your public relations program. Chapter Seven uses real-life case studies to show how the use of research in setting objectives, defining strategy and tactics, and evaluation work together in practice to achieve three kinds of results: generating revenue, doing more with less through superior performance, and avoiding costs altogether.

Chapter Eight shows how you can put the lessons of this book to work for you, explains why you need to do it now, and counters some common misapprehensions about using research and measurable objectives.

Audience

This book holds value for everyone in public relations—and especially in media relations—in corporations, agencies, nonprofits, and government organizations around the world. It also provides insights for corporate communicators and those in advertising and marketing, from the chief marketing officer on down. And it offers specific guidance to senior executives who oversee PR departments. In fact, each chapter concludes with a set of questions that every marketing and PR investment decision maker should ask.

Seizing the Future

Professionals who continue to practice publicity and corporate communications as they have in the past will find that they are dinosaurs in the new environment. On the other hand, those who face up to or even embrace the need for change and adopt scientific research methods to systematically and methodically plan and evaluate public relations programs will find a bright future ahead.

Acknowledgments

An endeavor such as this is a culmination of support from many corners:

First and foremost, I'm grateful for Nancy, Graham, and Cameron, whose love, patience, and understanding are my keystone. I'm also thankful for the support and guidance of my parents and sister, Lesley.

These acknowledgments would not be complete without recognizing the colleagues with whom and through whom I've learned so much: Lisa Binzel, Wayne Bullock, KC Brown, Norman Clements, Mary Durkin, Craig Mitchell, and Beth Roed. Also, thanks go to my comrades in Norwalk, Portsmouth, Washington, Chicago, and London.

Special respect must be paid to our Delahaye clients, past and present, whose desire to elevate the PR function created us and whose curiosity continues to inspire us.

Through the years, we've been lucky to be affiliated with great companies: Bacon's Information and Observer, Delahaye's current parent, which provided encouragement during the authoring process; Medialink, which provided Delahaye with an environment in which to take root and to grow; and Copernicus, which provided me with direction, purpose, and a sense of what is possible in the field of research-based PR consulting.

This book could not have become a reality without the vision of the IABC's Natasha Spring, who saw the makings of a book at the heart of a conversation. Thanks also to Alan Shrader, who as my editor provided guidance and empathy; Kathe Sweeny, who fostered the ideative process; and Bruce Jeffries-Fox, who as a friend and mentor provided great assistance during the finalization process.

April 2006   MARK WEINER
Norwalk, Connecticut

The Author

MARK WEINER is president of Delahaye, the world's most prestigious provider of public relations research, analysis, and consulting. After its founding in 1994 as Medialink Research, the firm acquired The Delahaye Group in 1999, adopted its name, and then became Delahaye in its current form. Delahaye is based in Norwalk, Connecticut, with offices in Portsmouth, New Hampshire; Chicago, Illinois; Washington, D.C.; and London, England, with affiliates around the world. The firm provides research-based consulting in areas related to public relations, marketing, and corporate reputation and employee communications, with client engagements in forty countries. Delahaye's research is used by the world's leading companies to set objectives; develop strategy; and evaluate the performance of how their communication initiatives affect the attitudes, understanding, and behaviors of their target audiences. The firm currently employees a hundred researchers and analysts, who provide a range of attitudinal research, traditional and new media content analysis, and statistical modeling services.

Since he entered the field in 1986, Weiner has been a frequent conference speaker and a regular contributor to leading professional journals, sitting on the editorial advisory boards of PRSA's *Strategist* and *PR News*. In addition, he was the 2004 chair of the Measurement Commission of the Institute for Public Relations. He is a member of the International Association of Business Communicators, the Public Relations Society of America, and the Institute for Public Relations. Before public relations, Weiner was an editor and syndicated newspaper columnist with the McNaught Newspaper Syndicate after starting his career with the *New York Times* News Service.

Unleashing the Power of PR

Part One

THE CHANGING LANDSCAPE OF MARKETING AND CORPORATE COMMUNICATION

1

New Opportunities for Marketing and Public Relations

In recent years, more companies in industries ranging from auto manufacturing to financial services and from consumer packaged goods to entertainment have reached the same unexpected conclusion: PR works. And at times, PR works better than other forms of marketing and at a small fraction of the cost.

Professional communicators have been using PR to deliver value for decades. What's new is that a handful of leading professionals are now scientifically proving how they are generating measurable benefits from their public relations activities. The progress that this change represents is significant: rather than relying on subjective perceptions of what represents value, they are applying the concept of "return on investment" (ROI—a term that has long been used by financial professionals) and objectively measuring the economic benefits of public relations activity against its associated costs. When someone asks about the ROI of an investment, he or she is really asking, "How much money did I make (or lose) in relation to what I spent?" And the answer to this question is conveyed in the language of business, not that of perceptions.

One element of PR-ROI is to scientifically show a contribution to sales. The first documented case of this form of PR-ROI analysis came during the course of an extensive and sophisticated statistical analysis of marketing performance in 1999, when telecommunications giant AT&T discovered an amazing fact: public relations, in the form of media relations, generated just as many new long-distance customers as advertising, even though the company invested substantially more resources in advertising than in PR. What's more, the analysis showed that public relations regularly provided a boost to other forms of marketing: when news about AT&T was positive, prominent, and highly visible, advertising was more successful, outbound telemarketing was more productive, and inbound telemarketing was more effective. The discovery changed the way AT&T marketers worked with PR professionals to plan for and evaluate overall marketing effectiveness.

In more recent years (prior to the company's acquisition by and absorption into SBC to become "the new AT&T"), AT&T's position as one of the world's dominant companies was in decline. The example of AT&T offers two important lessons: the first is that public relations is a greatly undervalued resource that not only performs well in its own right but also adds value to other forms of marketing communication. The second is that while public relations opens the doors to a great many forms of opportunity, no amount of positive PR can overcome the harmful effects of deregulation, flawed business strategy, and intense—and even unscrupulous—competition. Nevertheless, like so many "firsts" uncovered throughout its history, AT&T was the first company to accurately measure the interaction and effect of public relations within the marketing mix. As a result of AT&T's work, it could never again be said that PR is "soft" when it comes to making a measurable contribution toward an organization's achievement of meaningful business outcomes.

As explored in greater detail in later chapters, research proving the surprising power of public relations is being replicated at other companies and is creating new opportunities for PR in corporate communication and brand marketing. Public relations is unique within the marketing and communications mix, and it is my aim to show how PR can take a more central role in the way companies and brands evoke meaningful business outcomes through marketing and communication. In this chapter, I outline seven elements of change that have altered the landscape of corporate and marketing communication. These elements set the stage for public relations to achieve a special degree of primacy:

- Transformations in the media business
- Declining impact of traditional mass marketing
- Changing media consumption habits
- Access, abundance, and speed of information
- Decreasing brand loyalty
- Increasing distrust of large corporations
- Increasing levels of accountability

These factors create new opportunities for public relations that are now being found in the quickly shifting landscape in which marketers and communicators must operate.

Transformations in the Media Business

Throughout the history of American marketing and communication, traditional media have played a central role of delivering information, whether it was paid for or not. Whether the medium was an eighteenth-century newspaper, a nineteenth-century magazine, twentieth-century radio and television, or twenty-first-century Internet, the symbiosis between media and marketing is inextricable. But the media environment is in a state of constant change, and with this change comes opportunity.

Fierce competition, the rise of the Internet and other forms of new media, lower advertising revenues, and other pressures are leaving many media companies on the run. These companies are cutting costs and cutting staff in editorial departments and newsrooms in broadcast and print media. Like employees at many organizations, journalists and editors are asked to deliver more with less and for less. Many have turned to using nationally syndicated columnists and news services rather than staff writers and editors. Since syndicated material and news services cost money, many editors look to public relations departments and agencies as a source of news and feature material, creating new opportunities from the emerging synergies between the journalist and the PR professional.

A related trend also presents opportunities. While many journalistically driven media (think *New York Times* and CBS *Network News*) have clear separation between advertising and editorial, others do not. This provides for new opportunities for marketers. For example, a Delahaye survey among editors at women's beauty magazines in eleven countries in North America, South America, Western Europe, and Asia indicated that when it comes to writing a feature on a particular beauty-care category, lipstick, for example, the first phone calls for background information are to the magazine's biggest advertisers.

The result of this fuzziness is that marketers now seek to combine PR's ability for engaging storytelling with advertising's power to control frequency and timing. Savvy marketers work with broadcast PR consultants like Medialink, which produces video news releases and other video assets used by TV news programs, to counter the threat of TiVo by producing thirty-second spots delivered in the form of clearly identifiable programming content (as opposed to "news" content). For example, a movie channel may be showing *Rain Man*, which features a classic 1949 Buick Roadmaster convertible being driven across America by Tom Cruise and Dustin Hoffman. Prior to running more easily conventional (and TiVo-able) advertising spots, Buick may run a thirty-second "Did You Know?" featurette spotlighting Buick's rich legacy in film. The content is engaging and informational, it's relevant to those who have just been watching the movie's lead characters race across the country in the classic car, and it keeps viewers glued to the set rather than fast-forwarding ads or running to the refrigerator. This marketing form delivers the involvement and credibility that advertisers envy and public relations regularly provides. In fact, most of the advertising of this type is created and procured by PR people as often as advertising departments and agencies.

The Decline of Traditional Mass Marketing

According to the investment firm Veronis Suhler Stevenson Partners LLC (VSS) in their 2004 "Communications Industry Forecast," the total U.S. expenditures on trade marketing and trade promotion, advertising, and consumer promotion are more than $800 billion annually. From 1999 to 2004, spending grew at a rate of 5.2 percent per year. With forecast spending increasing to an annual compound rate of 6.7 percent, total marketing spending will exceed $1 trillion by 2009.

With a trillion dollars at stake, two enormously compelling questions marketers now face are "What is the relative effectiveness of my spending?" and "What is the predictability and propriety of my allocation of spending across the marketing mix?" And with so much money on the table, it's no wonder that marketers are under severe pressure to achieve the biggest impact for the lowest cost, an imperative that plays to the strengths of public relations.

Jim Stengel, marketing chief at Procter & Gamble, stated (in his address to attendees at the annual meeting of the American Association of Advertising Agencies in February 2004), "Today's marketing model is broken. We're applying antiquated thinking and work systems to a new world of possibilities." But Stengel's concerns are just the latest in a litany of doubt where marketing effectiveness is concerned. Commenting on the effectiveness of his advertising, early-twentieth-century retailer John Wanamaker is famously quoted as saying, "Half the money I spend on advertising is wasted. The trouble is, I don't know which half."

Board members, investors, and employees are looking for something better than "trust me," and with the amounts of money being spent on uncertain returns, they deserve it. The challenge implicit in the concerns expressed by top executives is simple: "Get meaningful results for my marketing and communication investment." PR can deliver such results in measurable ways, and can prove its value with ROI metrics powerful enough to satisfy the most demanding CFO.

Public relations helps in many ways. For example, studies have shown that a favorable brand environment shaped through positive, prominent, and highly visible news coverage provides a lift for price promotions and other forms of marketing. Post Cereal, a division of food giant Kraft Foods, provides a case in point. Post chose to lower the cost of its cereals significantly simply by eliminating expensive coupon promotions. At the time, increasing amounts of scrutiny were being brought to bear on the cereal manufacturers as the price of a box of cereal was steadily rising while the cost of its ingredients—primarily sugar, corn syrup, and grain—were either declining or flat. Congressional hearings were called.

Coincidentally, while the decision required serious marketing consideration, the announcement was made through Kraft's public relations department. The news appeared on the front page of many opinion-leading newspapers and received widespread coverage. In the absence of any advertising or in-store promotions, the brand's market share jumped by several points within weeks of the PR announcement. After early criticism of their leading-edge competitor, Kellogg's and General Mills soon followed Post's example by announcing reduced promotions within the year. Interestingly, just as soon as Kellogg's and General Mills announced their delayed initiatives (again using media relations–based PR), Post Cereal was given a supplementary shot in the arm as every news item covering the price reductions by its much larger competitors drew attention to the cereal price-promotion pioneer, and Post was a beneficiary. Post's elimination of price promotion at the time was considered to have provided an immediate sales boost; the cost of the media relations campaign was basically the cost of a press conference, a few press releases, and the PR agency, which could be estimated to be, at most, a tiny fraction of the multimillion-dollar lift in sales that it triggered.

Referring again to the Veronis Suhler analysis, public relations (at between $3 and $4 billion annually) represents a barely noticeable part of marketing expenditure. (See Table 1.1.) But with its unique ability to tell an organization's story credibly and engagingly

Table 1.1. Communications Industry Segments Ranked by Five-Year Growth.

Segment	1999–2004		2004–2009	
	CAGR (percent)*	Rank	CAGR (percent)*	Rank
Consumer Internet	24.6	1	14.5	1
Custom Publishing	13.6	2	12.1	2
Cable and Satellite Television	9.9	3	7.5	6
Public Relations	7.8	4	8.9	3
Branded Entertainment	7.0	5	8.2	4
Entertainment Media	5.8	6	7.0	7
Professional and Business Information Services	5.4	7	7.8	5
Direct Marketing	4.8	8	6.0	9
Out-of-Home Advertising	3.8	9	5.5	12
Yellow Pages	3.8	10	4.6	15
Educational and Training Media	3.4	11	5.2	13
Broadcast and Satellite Radio	2.8	12	6.2	8
Broadcast Television	2.7	13	4.3	17
Business-to-Business Promotion	2.6	14	5.7	11
Consumer Promotion	2.5	15	4.9	14
Consumer Books	1.8	16	2.1	19
Consumer Magazines	1.0	17	4.5	16
Newspapers	0.6	18	2.8	18
Business-to-Business Media	−0.1	19	5.8	10

*Compound annual growth rate.

Source: Veronis Suhler Stevenson Partners LLC

at very low cost, media relations–based PR is getting more and more attention within the marketing and communication mix, with forecast spending on the increase. (See Table 1.2.)

And sophisticated statistical analysis is demonstrating PR's value. *Marketing mix modeling* is an analytical approach that identifies and quantifies the marketing elements that impact behavior in the short term. These models are built using multiple regression analysis, a statistical procedure that relates changes in marketing mix and base factors to weekly changes in sales. In dozens of cases across a dozen industries using this technique, media relations–based PR has demonstrated a quantifiable ability to deliver incremental revenue on a par with advertising but at a cost that is far lower than that of advertising and promotions.

Changing Media Consumption Habits

One challenge facing traditional marketers is how people get their information. As noted, the media and advertising businesses are feeling the pinch of these phenomena. The Simultaneous Media Usage Study conducted by BIGresearch evaluated media usage among the U.S. population through 2003. The methodology was very thorough, including three waves of interviewing through which more than thirty thousand responses were analyzed. The study revealed that media usage includes little discrete viewing, reading, or listening. In other words, very few people are paying full attention to any particular medium at any given time. What was more, *individuals* engage with the media rather than *households*: generally speaking, everyone in the household is a media user but they are all doing it on their own, in their own way, and typically using more than one form of media at a time—whether it is reading a magazine while watching TV or talking on the phone while listening to the radio. In this context, attention is a form of currency, and those forms of communication that command attention drive the value equation.

Table 1.2. Communications Industry Segments Ranked by Size.

Segment	2004		2009	
	$ Millions	*Rank*	*$ Millions*	*Rank*
Direct Marketing	135,367	1	180,978	1
Professional and Business Information Services	97,822	2	142,325	2
Cable and Satellite Television	93,376	3	134,220	3
Entertainment Media	88,564	4	124,349	4
Newspapers	63,527	5	72,926	6
Broadcast Television	43,176	6	53,251	8
Business-to-Business Promotion	41,658	7	54,957	7
Consumer Internet	37,552	8	74,038	5
Consumer Promotion	31,639	9	40,206	9
Consumer Magazines	22,452	10	27,936	12
Custom Publishing	22,009	11	38,881	10
Business-to-Business Media	20,911	12	27,684	13
Branded Entertainment	20,729	13	30,724	11
Broadcast and Satellite Radio	20,306	14	27,449	14
Consumer Books	19,761	15	21,903	16
Educational and Training Media	18,694	16	24,037	15
Yellow Pages	15,928	17	19,973	17
Out-of-Home Advertising	5,834	18	7,623	18
Public Relations	3,410	19	5,212	19

Source: Veronis Suhler Stevenson Partners LLC

When consumers were asked what *advertising-driven* communication influences their purchase decisions, Network Television finishes on top:

What Influences Purchase Decisions?

Medium	Percent
Network TV	15.3
Cable TV	12.4
Radio	9.3
Newspapers	8.2
Yellow pages	5.3
Magazines	5.1
E-mail	3.0
Outdoor	2.1
Word-of-mouth	30.8
Coupons	24
Read an article	17.7

However, the power of advertising is exceeded by "word of mouth" and "read an article," and here is where public relations can shine. To illustrate the power of PR, consider again the example of AT&T in which sophisticated marketing mix analysis revealed that while most new customers came as a result of outbound telemarketing and direct marketing, public relations generated just as many new customers as did mass-market advertising (see Figure 1.1.). And public relations provided a lift to other forms of marketing that was not reciprocal: when the news about AT&T was positive, the advertising, direct marketing, and telemarketing were more effective as a result. But increased advertising or telemarketing provided no carryover benefit to the other marketing agents.

Even more startling was the ROI: when AT&T compared the cost-per-customer-won figures for telemarketing, direct marketing,

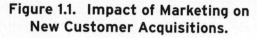

**Figure 1.1. Impact of Marketing on
New Customer Acquisitions.**

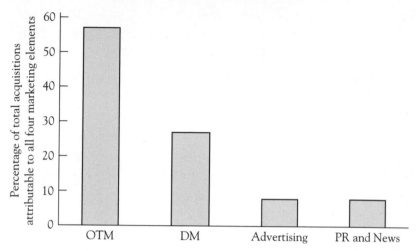

advertising, and PR, PR was shown to deliver results at a small fraction of the cost of other marketing agents. The figures are striking:

Cost per Acquisition by Channel

Cost per acquisition via outbound telemarketing:	$63
Cost per acquisition via targeted inbound telemarketing:	$103
Cost per acquisition via nontargeted inbound telemarketing:	$47
Cost per acquisition via advertising:	$95
Cost per acquisition via PR and news:	$15

While people may be on the phone when reading the newspaper, the news content in the paper commands a higher level of
involvement than most advertising does. So in a time when companies of all stripes are starving for proven and viable marketing
investments in the face of declining returns from mass-market
advertising, PR has demonstrated that not only is it worthy of significant marketing dollars, it makes other marketing investments
more viable, as well.

Access, Abundance, and Speed of Information

Vast amounts of news and information are available to audiences today, and you can expect ever-increasing quantities of information at accelerated speeds in the future. What is more, this abundance presents an increased need for understanding and perspective as the Internet, for example, provides equal access to so many perspectives on a single subject: unmediated opposition and motivated enemies alike compete with bona fide sources of news as well as the organization's own Web site. Most consumers are not savvy enough to differentiate genuine news from rumor, propaganda, and oppositional agendas. With the need for constant vigilance, public relations serves most companies as their sword and their shield: PR departments around the globe monitor all forms of news and information for the emergence of relevant stories so that threats may be addressed and so that opportunities may be leveraged.

Around the world and around the clock, millions of people feel the need to keep abreast of events as they happen. The ever-quickening pace of life has already drawn audiences from traditional media to the continuity of twenty-four-hour cable news networks and the accessibility of the Web. As issues arise, the production cycles of most advertising and mass marketing prohibit timely participation in the debate. Even many traditional news sources find it difficult to engage. Of all forms of corporate and marketing communication, public relations stands alone in its ability to quickly frame issues through dialogue, thus providing a degree of responsiveness and context that most examples of paid media cannot (but that consumers need).

While most of this chapter is devoted to external audiences, an interesting aspect of these heightened levels of information access is the impact on employees. In their efforts to attract and retain quality staff members, companies invest in employee relations and employee communications initiatives. Most commonly, employee communications departments rely on the monthly or quarterly employee newsletter, the company closed-circuit television, and e-mail updates. But employee communications surveys we've conducted indicate a growing sense of mistrust toward employers, especially big companies, and so company-controlled communication vehicles are not seen as the most credible sources for understanding. People's search for contextual information about their employer (and sometimes their own security for future employment with that employer) depends heavily on the grapevine. After word of mouth, employees often look to the Internet and other sources where a wide variety of viewpoints are found but where journalistic standards for balanced reporting may be lost.

This is also true for journalists, who have a professional responsibility for fair, unbiased reporting. Toward that goal, journalists often feature third-party commentary and opposing viewpoints. Easy access is afforded through the Web, not just for sources and opinion makers but also for new story ideas and for historical news coverage.

As the public liaison for most organizations, PR stands to gain in the new atmosphere of access, abundance, and velocity by being a reliable and proactive source from the start. When PR has arranged for an abundance of positive or at least balanced information in the bank in the form of third-party news coverage, employees and journalists are much more likely to find balanced, contextual reporting by which they can make sense of the questions they have in a way that house-organs and advertising cannot replicate.

Decreasing Brand Loyalty

Throughout my life, I have known my mother to eat only Kellogg's Rice Krispies, and to drink only Chase & Sanborn coffee. I, on the other hand, will buy whichever cereal is on sale and sweet enough for my kids to want to eat, and whatever coffee is being brewed at local gas-station convenience stores. The different levels of brand loyalty represented by Mother's preferences and my own are being played out in millions of transactions every day. The economic impact is extraordinary. As consumers, we've been trained by marketers to follow incentives, wait for the sale, and use coupons . . . *just show us the money*. But this is not to say that brand loyalty is impossible to achieve; it just needs to be created in new ways using all the tools available, particularly public relations. Unlike promotions and advertising, PR is a very powerful agent for engendering loyalty by shaping a brand as more than a product—as something that reflects one's beliefs and life priorities.

One form of loyalty building is known as "cause-related marketing," which can be defined as the public involvement of a for-profit company with a nonprofit organization with the dual purpose of promoting the company's product or service and providing financial support for the nonprofit.

Popular brands often pursue this strategy. Avon supports finding a cure for breast cancer, Liz Claiborne supports ending violence against women, Staples supports assisting needy children with school supplies. Each of these campaigns relies heavily on public relations as a key vehicle for promoting the brand, but more important, for communicating with target audiences as to what the brand *represents*. Because these are sensitive messages that can be difficult to communicate genuinely through mass-market advertising or cents-off coupons, organizations look to the media, with their third-party imprimatur, to convey a greater trust and understanding of the issues and the brands with which they are tied. In addition to building loyalty among customers, cause-related marketing programs also build loyalty among employees and other constituencies.

The phrase "cause-related marketing" was first used by American Express in 1983 to describe its campaign to raise money for the restoration of the Statue of Liberty. American Express made a one-cent donation to the restoration of the Statue of Liberty every time someone used its charge card. According to onPhilanthropy.com, a global resource for nonprofit and philanthropy professionals, the number of new users soon grew by 17 percent. Public relations was a primary vehicle during the campaign.

The May 11, 2005, issue of *Retail Merchandiser* tells how Staples, the office supplies superstore, in addition to providing generous financial support, donated nearly $100,000 worth of school supplies to the Kids in Need program. Tom Nutile, VP of public relations for Staples, said, "Our mission at Staples is to serve our customers. We like to support those causes that not only do great things in our community but also assist us in branding our company and aligning the good works that we do every day—helping businesses to grow, helping teachers, helping students—and through the Kids in Need Foundation, we have found a real philanthropic partner. Together, we can make a positive impact in our communities."

Not all PR-driven loyalty programs are built around charitable giving. A perfect example is Harley-Davidson, whose public relations is used to reinforce the brand and thus stimulate sales. Harley-Davidson enjoys an unrivaled level of connectedness with its motorcycle customers. It's been said that if a true measure of brand loyalty is the number of customers with logo tattoos, Harley-Davidson would be a sure winner. The company has a legendary brand and, through applied public relations, generates ample volumes of press coverage. Recently, in the face of an aging customer base, the company used public relations as a means of reaching an adjacent target market—women—to expand its brand without diluting its image. It won't be long before our moms and the girl next door will be brandishing the black-and-orange Harley-Davidson shield.

Increasing Distrust of Large Corporations

Recent years have witnessed an unprecedented level of public scrutiny, which has led to an enormous backlash against large corporations. And it's not just the most visible bad boys like Enron and WorldCom. Intense focus on these infamous companies shone the spotlight on their accounting firms as well as on some perfectly spotless companies that just happened to be within their sectors. The economic impact of corporate mistrust is incalculable. There are also political implications. The Sarbanes-Oxley Act legislates corporate oversight at the federal government level. And legal implications and costs continue to rise in the form of class-action suits.

The opportunity for public relations is clear: in an environment where the stakes have never been higher in terms of criminalized CEOs, determined attorneys general, unparalleled levels of activism, and amplified liability, public relations is one corporate communication vehicle that, by definition, engages and promotes dialogue. The more a company can communicate openly, genuinely, consistently, and visibly, the greater its chances of weathering the storm, but more important, of avoiding the storm front altogether. As a result, public relations becomes a means of managing goodwill, an extremely valuable asset during times of intense scrutiny.

PR executives at top companies are much more than highly paid publicists; they are extremely important and trusted advisers. And because it is the role of public relations to represent the public's interests in corporate strategy and execution, PR execs are often the source of independent thinking toward corporate ethics and values. In this way, companies look to public relations departments to build trust and connectedness with their constituents.

Increasing Levels of Accountability

While many opportunities originate outside the organization, the demand within corporations for every department to deliver a positive ROI presents interesting opportunities for PR. Given the issues that companies face now and detailed earlier in this chapter—a changing media environment, difficulties for mass marketers, and so on and on—and the high levels of expenditure, marketers are under intense pressure to deliver. In light of the challenge to deliver meaningful business outcomes like sales, PR holds promise for those who look to deliver more with less and for less, but with certainty. And while accountability for some highly funded marketing is challenging, PR is able to scientifically measure its impact and value in undeniable ways.

As explored in the second part of the book, public relations can be measured in ways that bring as high a level of accountability as any other form of marketing. Using available tools and methods, PR people are already in the position to set measurable goals and to report on their progress in meeting or exceeding these goals. Simple and accessible measures such as "volume of news coverage versus goal," "percentage of all coverage coming from key markets," and "percentage of coverage containing at least one key message" are practical and affordable, and even if they don't make a strict connection to ROI, they do indicate to those in the C-suite that at least PR monies are being spent wisely.

Seizing the Opportunity

This chapter makes the case for public relations and the many factors that now support PR within the marketing and communication mix. At the same time, these opportunities come with unique challenges, which are explored in Chapter Two. But even with challenges, some of which are significant, the changes now driving opportunity are happening with you or without you. Those who embrace these opportunities will thrive. And while those who adapt will survive, those who choose to ignore them will certainly fade away.

Questions Every Marketing and PR Investment Decision Maker Should Ask

- Have we assessed the transformations currently under way in the media business? If so, how are we capitalizing on them?

- Are we generating an appropriate, measurable return on our investment in traditional mass marketing? How do we know?

Continues

- How are we taking advantage of the changing media consumption habits of our customers?
- Given the increased access, abundance, and speed of information in current society, how are we making the most of our opportunities?
- What is the extent of our customers' loyalty to our brand? What are we doing to improve it?
- Do our customers trust us? What do we need to do to earn even greater levels of trust?
- What is the reputation of our organization? What are we doing to improve our reputation among key constituencies?
- What controls do we have in place to ensure that our marketing initiatives can be measured and held accountable? How do we apply what we learn from the process to make even better decisions in the future?

2

New Challenges Facing
Marketing and Public Relations

With PR's increased visibility comes the need to generate and demonstrate a positive ROI as well as a satisfactory *return on expectation*. In other words, public relations faces numerous challenges on a number of different levels. From within the organization, PR budgets have always been given great scrutiny—meaning, kept as small as feasible, and sometimes smaller—and yet the expectation is that PR will provide a return on investment for every dollar spent. In addition, conventional marketing wisdom holds that PR is "soft" and doesn't deserve a substantial share of resources because it can't be measured. Environmentally, PR is under pressure to deal effectively with the proliferation of new media and new media categories, globalization, and the close examination of company actions based on the growing distrust for large organizations. And finally, from within, the public relations profession places obstacles in its own path, such as loosely defined professional standards, generally inadequate levels of professional education and talent development, and the self-perpetuation of the myth that PR can't be measured scientifically.

Internal Challenges

The internal challenges include conventional marketing wisdom that often boxes PR efforts into old formulas, constrictions of funding and resources, and the uncontrollability of information.

Conventional Marketing Wisdom

Conventional marketing wisdom often keeps PR on the periphery.

Within most organizations, PR is regarded as great for interacting with the media, writing and distributing press releases, and helping with special events, but not much else. However, the sphere and potential of public relations is much greater than top management often perceives. Whether it is raising awareness among prospective hires about a company's being a desirable place to work or on Wall Street as being a worthwhile investment, or creating marketing momentum to accelerate the sale of goods and services, public relations is capable of some very heavy lifting.

But conventional wisdom often gets in the way. Consider the case of an imported luxury car manufacturer with limited advertising resources. Most domestic car publicity is generated during the major U.S. car-show season, which begins in Los Angeles in January and lasts for just a few short months. During this time of year, extraordinary amounts of news coverage emanate from these shows and the new cars and concepts introduced there. For this car company, every new model was a home run, with coverage that was consistently positive, prominent, and widely visible. In fact, the coverage was so consistently positive that it began to feel as controllable as advertising.

Taking into account the company's high sales volume during this time of high PR productivity, the company's marketing and PR leadership debated their opportunity to reallocate its limited advertising budget from a twelve-month spend to a more intensive eight-month spend. In this way, the PR leadership reasoned, a higher level of visibility could be sustained without increased spending through the managed use of PR during the high-visibility months of the car shows, and through advertising during the post–car-show period when publicity was more difficult to deliver on such a large scale. During the course of the analysis, the car company's advertising agency did everything it could do to fight the reallocation (that's *reallocation*, not a reduction) of advertising spending. In the end, the discussion was squelched, the PR leadership buckled, and the company continued down its conventional path. Could the luxury car importer have accomplished much more with a more balanced marketing approach that included a strategic use of PR? Unfortunately, the company was never able to test this proposition because it deferred to the self-interests of small-minded people. Had it taken this step forward at that time, it might have become one of the first companies to quantify PR's ability to drive sales.

In other cases, public relations visibly helps deliver sales, especially with products that require high levels of research and consideration (like a new car) and in those cases where news coverage generates a lot of visibility (like new car introductions at the major car shows).

Consider the case of a German luxury import car company, which conducted regular advertising tracking studies that month after month reported consistent levels of awareness. At the same time, the company conducted PR tracking research in the form of quarterly media content analyses through which it tracked the quantity and quality of news generated about its cars. Suddenly and without explanation, the company started receiving calls about a new model upgrade that hadn't been advertised. Consumer momentum for the car was building through the slightest hint of prelaunch commentary and unauthorized photography appearing in auto-buff magazines. It was the auto-buff reporting that was creating such high levels of excitement and anticipation. The company's PR team chose to leverage the momentum through a more formal PR plan. In the end, the impact of the news coverage among the company's fans was so great that by the time the new model was officially on the market, the model's annual limited production run was already sold out. The company never spent a penny on any form of marketing other than media relations and PR. Without the research, it would have been difficult to identify and then trace the news coverage from its origins until it reached the tipping point, but with it, the company was able to use what it had learned to its advantage in its subsequent car launches.

Resources and Funding

Generally speaking, one of PR's key benefits is that it is intrinsically less costly than advertising: PR requires no money-back offers and no media buys, so even its most ardent practitioners *want* it to have a smaller budget. That being the case, it would be unrealistic to expect that PR would ever have the same budget as advertising. In its annual Communications Industry Forecast, first mentioned in Chapter One, VSS predicts that PR spending will rise at a rate of roughly 9 percent between 2004 and 2009, a healthy pace of growth.

But still, even as marketers begin to recognize PR's abilities, public relations is grossly underfunded when compared to other marketing forms, ranking dead last by VSS in terms of communications industry spending. Compared to direct marketing, which commands the largest outlay at approximately $135 billion in 2004, PR expenditure is almost invisible: about $3.4 billion, roughly 2 percent of direct marketing spending. When factored by the total communications spend of $800 billion, PR spending rounds down to 0 percent.

One consumer products company spends 70 percent of its marketing budget on mass market television advertising, 29 percent of its marketing on trade advertising, and 1 percent on PR: that's a ratio of 70:1 in favor of TV advertising over PR.

To properly deliver consistent and effective public relations results, PR programs must be properly funded. PR spending appeared to be on the upswing in 2004 as compared to previous years, according to the third annual PR Generally Accepted Practices (GAP) Study, conducted by The University of Southern California's Strategic PR Center and sponsored by the Council of PR Firms, but "one year doesn't make a trend," as Jerry Swerling, director at the Center, says. Interestingly, the study suggested a new area of vibrancy and maturity for the PR profession: in nearly all organizational sectors, respondents indicated that their CEOs believe that PR is the number one contributor to organizational success, ahead of functions such as marketing, finance, legal, sales, and others. (PR was ranked sixth out of eight functions in both 2002 and 2003.) What's more, among Fortune 1000 companies, PR is the only corporate function to have increased in value to the organization in each year since the GAP study was initiated in 2002.

The study goes on to say that among *Fortune* magazine's "Most Admired Companies," PR budgets are bigger at an average of $9.2 million versus average spending at all other companies of $3.8 million. Obviously, bigger companies would logically have bigger budgets, but the most admired companies have proportionately bigger PR budgets than companies of similar size. So, in a time when PR is considered to be of growing and primary importance, and when spending is up, why is PR still relatively underfunded within the marketing and communications mix?

Three reasons: unwillingness among PR people to measure and thereby prove value and ROI; inability to scale with increased spending (even if you spent a hundred times the money on media relations, how many stories about mattresses can the media reasonably be expected to cover?), and conventional marketing wisdom, as discussed earlier.

The challenge for PR executives is to demonstrate value by *generating* value (the act of doing rather than simply telling). The key to both demonstrating and generating value is found in data, the language of business. The fundamental question for marketing and communication investors is, Why shift resources from advertising, a relatively risk-free investment with reliable though unspectacular performance, to PR, which appears more speculative? The necessary challenge for PR leadership is to provide proof of performance, whether asked to or not. Making the PR-to-sales connection in the form of marketing mix modeling, as discussed earlier, can be expensive, but tracking PR tactics and outputs can consist of a simple spreadsheet like the one in Figure 2.1, on which you monitor the number of placements, circulation and audience, tone, number of key messages delivered, and similar points. It doesn't have to cost a lot of money and it doesn't have to take a lot of time, but it does provide a nominal gauge of activity and performance in a way that reduces perceived risk when asking others to allocate resources.

Figure 2.1. PR-to-Sales Spreadsheet.

Date	Media Name	Key Market	Circulation or Audience	Key Messages	Tone	Pix (Yes/No)	Prominence	Dominance	First Mention

External Challenges

Public relations practitioners also face greater external challenges than ever before, including lack of control of the media, greater media attention to corporate behavior, and the rise of new forms of media, especially on the Internet.

Lack of Complete Control

Much of PR-driven communication and marketing is beamed through the lens of the journalist; especially in the case of media relations–oriented PR. Since it is the job of the journalists to be thorough and balanced in their reporting, public relations is semi-controllable at best, as shown in Figure 2.2. This is evidenced by the common situation of the senior executive who says, "Why do I keep seeing our competitors on the front cover of the trade journals when our company spends so much more on advertising?" In fact, each of the types of communication shown in the figure has its own effect; when managed properly and cohesively, each can contribute toward the achievement of real business outcomes.

Advertising, direct marketing, and Web sites, unlike media relations–centered PR, offer complete control over the frequency, positioning, and placement of key messages: you pay your money, and you've purchased the ability to control your message. Expensive as it is, this sort of "controlled communication" is more familiar and easier to understand for most executives, and so they tend to gravitate in that direction.

In contrast, a PR department can distribute a press release with high hopes, but has no guarantee that it will run as intended, if it appears at all. A recent *New York Post* story illustrates what can happen to even carefully crafted PR. The news item focused on the launch of a new product extension for a healthy kids' snack where wholesome apple sauce was married to explosive "Pop-Rock" candy. The story occupied half the page, featured a full-color photograph, and covered every detail of a new product launch. But the headline

Figure 2.2. Controlled, Semi-Controlled, and Uncontrolled Communication.

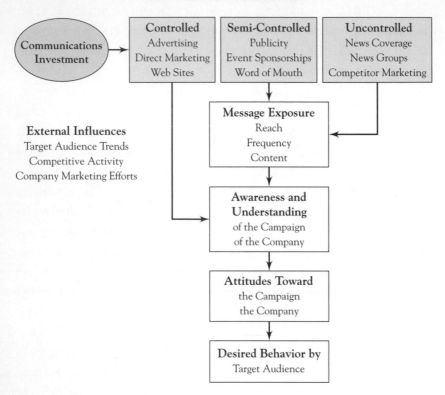

read, "Who Would Eat This Stuff?" The PR people seemed to do everything right: they attracted a major city daily to a product-launch press conference; they prepared a thorough press information kit, much of which (including the photo) was recognizable in the story; and they managed to generate very prominent news visible to hundreds of thousands of *New York Post* readers. But it wasn't the kind of coverage they were after. (Despite this unexpected result, PR people can professionally and ethically gain a level of control over the news-generating process; many of these techniques appear in Chapters Four, Five, and Six.)

Although it comes in several forms, "uncontrolled communication" in the world of news is often negative. In having to mitigate or respond to negative communication, the PR department is unique within the marketing mix. PR "owns the negative" within most organizations, and it becomes PR's job to manage the situation when the news is bad. Negative news can come from a variety of external and internal sources, but for PR professionals, negative news brings with it dual implications: on the plus side, these are the times when PR people prove their ability to provide expert counsel and leadership. On the minus side, particularly in cases where the negative news originates from bad corporate behavior, some wrong-headed executives mistakenly assume that PR should be used to "spin away" bad news rather than carefully examine the cause of the problem and address it.

Beyond the negative, the uncontrollability of public relations also stems from the nature of the news. During the period following the 9/11 attacks and then after the death of Pope John Paul, the news was almost entirely focused on the events of the day. As a result, public relations people either found that there was no news hole (time and space availability) for their initiatives to find a home in the media or they considered it to be wholly inappropriate to promote stories about a new chocolate chip cookie during a time of grieving. This is the character of the news and one of the primary difficulties facing PR planners.

Greater Scrutiny of Corporate Behavior

As noted in Chapter One, the growing distrust of corporations increases the need for effective public relations. But this distrust and greater scrutiny also make public relations more difficult. Because a good corporate reputation is earned, it requires three ingredients: good behavior, good performance, and the ability to communicate effectively. Some companies prefer to engage in one-way communication through corporate advertising rather than foster the dialogue through public relations in its largest context, including but not limited to media. Since a company's reputation is gauged by its publics rather than what an organization says about itself, self-promotional advertising can seem disingenuous or at least not credible when matters get truly serious. Martha Stewart's Web site promotion rang hollow following her indictment as it seemed so self-serving. Unfortunately, many CEOs seem to believe that the media are unimportant, easily manipulated or, even worse, the enemy, and this presents enormous challenges.

A variety of corporate communication elements can bring positive attention to a corporation, but PR is challenged with delivering positive perspective during extraordinarily difficult times. When the reputation of Wendy's was challenged by a hoaxster who claimed to have found a human finger in her Wendy's chili, the company used public relations to tell the company's side of the story, which was eventually proven to be true. Pepsi did the same during the syringe hoax in the late 1990s when it was reported that unsuspecting consumers found hypodermic needles in cans of Pepsi. These companies were the victims of hoaxes and PR played an important part in delivering effective messages relating to their innocence. However, sometimes companies *earn* negative attention by the bad decisions they've made—at which point, as mentioned earlier, it often falls to the PR person to clean up the mess. Not only does the PR department have to deal with the negative news, it must continue delivering counterbalancing positive news in areas other than those under scrutiny. So during a product recall, PR is used to communicate and demonstrate the company's capacity for leadership and corporate governance; for showing its connectedness with the community through philanthropic activity; and for promoting the company as being a good place to work and a corporation worthy of investment. This is no easy task.

Each year since 2000, the "Delahaye Index of Corporate Reputation" has tracked the way select opinion-leading print and broadcast media cover the hundred largest U.S.-based companies. Typically, the companies that generate the most positive and prominent news coverage perform well in more than one area. KC Brown, senior vice president of Research and Advisory Services at Delahaye, who created and oversees the "Index," theorizes that perceptions about a company (or a brand, for that matter) are shaped in two ways. The first is *direct experience*, whereby a person either works for a company, invests in it, or buys its products and services. The second form is *indirect experience*, such as news coverage, advertising, and word of mouth (see Figure 2.3). Indirect experience via media coverage is a primary means of learning about a company. Consider Enron: relatively few people had direct experience with it, but almost everyone has heard of it and has formed strong opinions as a result.

Corporate reputation can also present challenges to a particular company when its industry is under scrutiny or if even one member of the category is the subject of negative news. And the challenge cuts in two directions, as illustrated in the energy industry. Before its troubles were exposed, Enron was among America's most admired companies, held up as an example for others within the stodgier energy category. On the other hand, the Southern Company was criticized for being too conservative and unwilling to seize new opportunities by doing business "the Enron way." Southern's corporate communications and PR teams found it difficult to tell their

Figure 2.3. Shaping Public Perceptions.

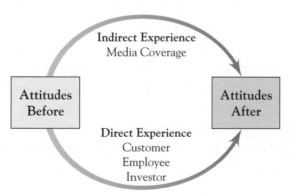

story in light of the Enron hoopla when Enron was on top. When Enron imploded, the entire energy industry was hurt by association. Every local news organization ran stories about their neighboring energy provider in relation to Enron, and many energy companies were wrongly associated with the troubled company. The energy firm that rebounded fastest was Southern, which had resisted the temptation to play by Enron's rules. To this day, Southern continues to be widely admired as a company yielding reliable and positive performance.

Even though PR and corporate communications departments don't necessarily drive corporate reputation (a company's financial performance is usually the key determinant among businesspeople, and its commitment to the community is the key determinant among people living nearby), it is the PR person who must manage the company's reputation regardless.

Given such high stakes and the many variables that can either help or hurt a reputation, it is imperative that companies do the research and evaluation that help to protect their good names. The good news is that a number of relatively inexpensive syndicated reputation studies are available at a fraction of the cost required to do them on a one-off, customized basis. Many companies participate in these studies, and in doing so, they underwrite the cost of each incremental participant. So for as little as $20,000 annually, a corporate communications department can track its own reputation as well as those of its competitors and peers. The best-known of the survey-based studies are *Fortune* magazine's "America's Most Admired Companies," the Reputation Institute and Harris Interactive's "Reputation Quotient," and the Delahaye Index, which analyzes the media's treatment of the top hundred U.S. companies. By tracking your own company in light of so many others, as found in each of these major endeavors, you have an opportunity to uncover opportunities for improvement by adapting to and adopting from the leaders, regardless of their industry and category.

New Media and Unmediated Media

Web logs (or blogs) were once the domain of techies seeking one another to discuss technology matters, but they and other forms of consumer-generated media (CGM) have emerged as powerful new alternatives to traditional media. Other forms of CGM are plentiful: podcasting, wikis, instant messaging, and smart mobs are some of the new players in a world where people are looking for the fastest way to receive, publish, and generate news on their own terms. The irony is that in many cases, these new media are, well, *unmediated*. "The State of the News Media 2005," published by the Project for Excellence in Journalism (www.journalism.org), stated that while once considered the guardian of truth, "The journalism of verification has ceded ground to a new journalism of assertion." This presents important challenges to PR pros who must now incorporate these niche media forms with traditional mass media within their overall media planning, even though the two media types play by entirely different rules.

The shift from a traditional, regimented, and centralized form of news to more participatory varieties represents profound changes in the way that information is communicated and the public's preferences for being communicated to: if you don't like the radio's play-list, create your own. If you don't like the content of traditional media, you can get your information from those with similar frustrations: if gossip found on "Page Six" of the *New York Post* is too bland, go to the Smoking Gun; if political coverage in the *Washington Post* is too tame, go to the Drudge Report.

The challenge to the public relations community is considerable as bloggers claim that they cannot be managed in the way that PR works with journalists to manage traditional media. Stories that originate in blogs face fewer obstacles than stories that originate in traditional media with journalistic standards. The more considerable challenge comes from the abundance of media and the speed with which they start up and shut down. One element of the PR pro's job is to stay ahead of the news by having insight into story preferences, editorial calendars, and who is where—and the sheer volume of elements to track has increased exponentially.

The key then is to monitor blogs and chat rooms to stay on top of the news. Even if bloggers, discussion group moderators, and chat rooms aren't warm to the traditional involvement of public relations, PR people can be useful contributors to responsible bloggers and moderators who recognize the responsibility for accuracy and who welcome participation as a way to advance their own point of view. PR people must keep abreast of developments so that they can be factored into traditional PR planning. In the case of one consumer product giant with whom Delahaye works, a rumor was circulating about a home-cleaning product and how it was poisoning pets in households using the product. Employing advanced techniques for acquiring, assessing, and acting upon these postings under the supervision of new media expert Mark Vangel, we helped the company not only quell the rumor but discover the perpetrator— who, when approached by our client, admitted to working for competitive interests. Upon the confrontation, the rumors ceased.

Self-Perpetuating Challenges

The field of public relations faces its own challenges as a profession. These include challenges relating to ethical standards, professional education, and perhaps most important of all, accountability.

Ethics and Credibility

Remarkably, in recent days, the public relations field has hit it big with front-page stories in the *New York Times*, the *Los Angeles Times*, and other "media of record." Unfortunately, the attention is not the kind one covets. Within quick succession, a series of stories broke that had a damaging impact on the profession's credibility and ethics. Fleishman-Hillard, one of PR's most admired agencies, was in the news for allegedly overbilling the Los Angeles Department of Water and Power, which raised questions about agency billing practices. The White House's use of phony press videos packaging political spin as news raised questions about whether laws against government-sponsored propaganda had been broken. Ketchum, another of PR's top agencies, was caught paying journalists as spokespeople, which raised questions about whether journalists' opinions were genuine or bought. All these cases undermine the credibility of a field that aspires to professional status. These events may seem extraordinary, but PR people face potentially similar hurdles every day.

Challenges to PR's credibility and ethics come in a variety of forms. For example, PR people are sometimes asked to overrepresent a product by using tactics that amount to misleading the public—yet one of the founding principles of PR is to tell the truth and to provide accurate information to our stakeholders. How many PR agencies are asked to promote products and services known to be inferior? How many PR people are asked to take sides on issues that put them in direct opposition to a healthy environment or in favor of a repressive government? How many times have PR people had to promote their company despite evidence of sweatshop labor in third-world countries? In a world with many options, how many PR people have deliberately chosen to act as if there is no winner unless there is a loser? The answer is that many PR people are either asked to or choose to participate in areas where the ethical standards are vague, at best.

On one hand, what PR elects to do or submits to doing is judged by the boss, by the company, by the company's publics, and by the general public. On the other hand, we have an obligation to our own conscience and the conscience of the profession as established by professional organizations like the International Association of Business Communicators (IABC) and the Public Relations Society of America (PRSA). In any case, the role of the public relations person is to represent the public's interest within the organization; when you are judged—as you will assuredly be judged—you are more likely to be in the right than in the wrong if you make it a matter of practiced principle to act in the public's interest.

In 1996 when speaking at MegaComm, Craig Miyamoto, a PRSA Fellow, described PR's "trilemma" (which is to say, a situation at least 50 percent more complicated than a simple dilemma) in the following way:

- As counselors, we need to know everything about a company, organization, or cause. This is indisputable. We cannot fulfill our responsibilities without this knowledge. And yet, because of our loyalties to our employer or client, we must keep it confidential. No matter how open and candid we wish to be, there are some things that must be kept in confidence.

- And yet, as the conscience of business, as the company's liaison with the public, we have a duty and obligation to reveal it to the public, even if we could lose our job or hurt others—including our own dear family members—in the process.

- Which brings us to a defining question for public relations practitioners: "What is the threshold beyond which an advocate may not ethically go?" Is there some point at which we can say, "It is ethical for me to do this one thing, but if I change this one particular element a mere 0.01 percent, does it then become unethical?" Where then is the line beyond which public relations counselors are morally obligated to sacrifice self and client for a larger social good? And if such a line exists, then how do we know when we've crossed it?

Now that there exists an elite group of public relations executives who have earned a seat at the policy-setting table, the challenge they face is in the choices they make regarding their individual power and their proximity to power.

Scientific public relations provides some structure upon which one can build more ethical and credible organizations. While research for and evaluation of PR is not intended to serve as a moral compass, it can provide some guidelines for ethical conduct—if only because one can better quantify the impact of others who have strayed from the moral path. Such observations permit risk—not to mention the very real penalties associated with these risks—to be identified and avoided. Companies like Enron and WorldCom always come up in these conversations, but if senior PR managers were able to contextualize the impact of the wrong-doing of these world-class bad guys, they might think twice (if shame and prison weren't enough). For example, in the "Delahaye Index of Corporate Reputation" of 2001, Enron ranked sixteenth among the hundred largest U.S.-based companies with the determinant Net Effect score of 185 million. One year later, when the company with the best reputation was Microsoft with a Net Effect score of 660 million, Enron was the worst company with a Net Effect score of –3.6 *billion*. In other words, the most negative score was of a magnitude six times worse than the highest positive score. Interestingly, to prove that reputation can be managed, financial-services giant AIG finished dead last in first-quarter 2005 release of the Delahaye Index, but by the third quarter, the company rose fifty places, the largest gain by any company during that time frame. To underscore a point made earlier in the chapter, the firm's rank improved not by spinning the media but by carefully examining its problems and by taking swift action to address them. In another example, Kmart finished third from the bottom in 2002 (due to financial problems rather than ethics). In the first quarter of 2005, it appeared in the top ten following its merger with Sears and Sears Holdings . . . an improvement of approximately *ninety* slots.

Professional Education and Talent Development

Each year, PR maven and newsletter publisher Jack O'Dwyer publishes his *Directory of Corporate Public Relations*, the bible for knowing who works where and other key information. And with every issue (in 2005 he celebrated the directory's thirty-fifth anniversary), he makes a point of counting the several hundred different titles under which PR people operate. If the field continues to be known under so many different names—external affairs, media relations, public relations, and corporate communications are but a few—how can we begin to distinguish the profession in a way that attracts and keeps the most talented people? Beyond the titles, University of Southern Alabama professor Don Wright asserts that the state of education in public relations can best be described as "conflicted": relatively few universities offer public relations courses; but the number of university PR classes is on the rise. At the same time the percentage of classes taught by qualified PR professors is going down; and very few PR educators are coming up through formal, educationally structured backgrounds. What is more, most of the people currently working in PR, especially in executive positions, have no formal education in PR at all and may not have aspired to work in PR when first starting out. While they may generally support the idea of a public relations curriculum, they may not see the need to hire PR majors out of school in the same way that the legal, medical, and accounting professions are drawn to those whose degrees are almost vocational and prerequisite.

Education in public relations suffers from many of the symptoms that ail the public relations profession overall: lack of visibility, lack of any compelling sense of primacy, lack of funding, and the rest. But as public relations evolves from its purely creative tradition to a future that balances art and science, and as universities prepare talent as well grounded in one as in the other, PR education will become more widely recognized as the source of the new breed of PR professional.

Accountability for Results

The science of public relations described in Chapter One is available to all public relations professionals through the application of public relations research and evaluation, but few PR people subscribe to these practices. This point was demonstrated by a survey conducted in 2003 among members of the preeminent Arthur Page Society by the Institute for Public Relations. The executives interviewed, who hold top positions at many of the world's most recognizable corporations and agencies, said the following:

- Research is an integral part of PR.
- Those who fund PR programs are demanding quantitative evaluation.
- PR people do not have a sufficient grasp of how to provide adequate proof of performance.
- The funding parties don't know enough about PR and how it should be measured to provide direction.
- Practitioners don't spend much money toward answering the effectiveness questions.

The result of the situation is that little progress is made.

What is more confounding is that many of the PR people who do choose to measure wind up using methods that are not considered by management to be particularly meaningful. Each year, Delahaye conducts hundreds of interviews with the senior executives who fund public relations programs in an effort to uncover the "secret value systems" in which PR must operate (these surveys, known as "Executive Audits," are discussed in greater detail in Chapter Three). What we see with great regularity is that executives who fund PR programs want PR programs to deliver on such measures as "raising awareness" and "delivering key messages to target media." The least favored measure among management is "volume of news coverage." Paradoxically, when PR people are asked to identify the measures they prefer, they generally answer "volume of news coverage"—the measure that their management values least.

Why don't more PR people measure? The excuses are many: "It's too expensive," "PR research and evaluation are too sophisticated for an organization our size," or "Executives within my organization trust me." As demands for accountability increase, those who rely on "trust me" are in for a rude awakening. And contrary to the belief that research and evaluation are oversophisticated and too expensive, most PR accountability programs can be done in-house inexpensively and simply. Even firms like Delahaye, who earn fees in excess of $1 million annually for sophisticated global measurement programs, have many more clients in the range of $2,000–$5,000 annually. While inexpensive programs may not be the most elaborate and advanced, they do provide assurance to PR's internal clients that things are going well, and that the PR budget is being spent wisely. And they provide enough insight to the PR people themselves to provide some guidance for improving results. In my opinion, most PR people choose not to measure for the simple reason that their bosses (or clients) aren't asking for it and the idea just doesn't appeal.

Unfortunately, the change to higher levels of accountability is happening whether PR people want it or not. In the end, if PR is to continue to advance, its ability to account for ROI, even in general or directional terms, will be called into question. And beyond accountability, PR research and evaluation enables PR people to create and execute smarter, more effective PR initiatives. The opportunity comes from taking the lead as an agent for positive change.

The practice of measurable, scientific public relations cannot take place in a vacuum: you must have a practical understanding of your situation and develop sensible plans. So the transition to accountability begins with asking questions and gathering information. Exhibit 2.1 provides the essentials.

Each of the eleven questions can be answered through means that range from the casual to the formal and from the conversational to the rigorous. With everything that's at stake—budgets, reputation, and overall business performance—the considerations are too great not to opt for the rigor and structure afforded through formal public relations research and analysis.

Exhibit 2.1. Eleven Questions You Must Ask Before Starting a Public Relations Program.

- *What are your organization's objectives?* The need to relate an organization's activities and investments to its overall goals and objectives is not confined to public relations, but *not doing so* is a surefire path to failure. Who cares, for example, if the PR department generates awareness for matters that fall outside the organization's purview? Ensuring that your objectives support the organization's is the surest way to avoid risk and to merchandise success, and the process for uncovering answers to this question is so easy that not to do so is, in a word, ridiculous. Chapter Three discusses the relatively simple and inexpensive course to discovery.

- *What are your department's objectives?* Just as it is essential for the PR department to support the overall organization's priorities, so too must the individual campaign strategy and tactics support the department's objectives. For example, in many organizations the primary PR objective is to stay *out* of the media. Generating a ton of coverage, which passes as the objective of most PR organizations, may be counterproductive in cases such as these. Not aligning your or your campaign's objectives to the department's is among the most direct ways to the unemployment line. And once again, answering this question is so easy, so accessible, that noncompliance is a form of professional malpractice. Chapter Four discusses the elements of strategy and tactics, each of which must support both the department and the organization as a whole.

- *What other programs are currently under way?* In the practice of public relations, which can affect such a wide range of areas within the organization, it is essential to have a firm grasp of what other initiatives—both communication programs and others—are in the works. Today's larger organizations are often so decentralized as to make coordination between departments almost impossible. But it is essential that you know what else might be in play and how these initiatives can affect one another.

- *What other departments will be affected?* In your quest for increased learning, you ought to determine the impact, if any, on other departments. To go through the complete public relations planning process without consideration for other departments and their respective planning and activities is to risk that your plans will be either less effective or, even worse, counterproductive as a result of what another department may be doing. Imagine the impact of a PR plan that emphasizes a theme like "corporate citizenship" at the same time that the company is moving jobs to Mexico. . . . If done in even slightly the wrong way, the potential for perceived disingenuousness is great. Especially when a simple conversation with peers

Exhibit 2.1. Eleven Questions You Must
Ask Before Starting a Public Relations Program, Cont'd.

in departments such as finance, human resources, advertising, and manufacturing is as easy as picking up the phone or walking down the hall. Consider the upside for working collaboratively, since public relations shares so much with other forms of marketing and communication.

- *How will you use the research findings?* While you may not know in advance every aspect of how the findings will be applied, you ought to have a hypothesis about what you hope to learn. Typical applications are *to set smarter objectives, to develop better messaging and media strategies*, and *to prove the value of* PR. Chances are, your applications will be a variation of one of these. If you work with an outside research provider, its staff can give more specific ideas based on their experiences with other clients. Examples appear throughout this book's chapters and the organizations whose experiences are described here are not that unlike those PR people experience every day.

- *Who are your target audiences?* Audience identification may well be the most important element in the entire communication planning process. Once the optimal audience is identified, the cycle for message development and media targeting becomes infinitely more precise and likely to succeed. Audience targeting is often underemphasized in the planning process, even though the risk for taking this critical step too lightly is enormous—especially since it doesn't have to involve rocket science or brain surgery, whichever you think is more difficult. Details are provided later in this chapter and examples appear throughout the book.

- *What are your key messages?* Most communicators enter the planning process with at least a sense of what they want to communicate, even if they don't opt for one of the scientific approaches to message development and message prioritization. PR research can reveal the extent to which your intended message is credible and is likely to resonate with your intended audience. Chapter Five discusses the process of "message engineering" in greater detail.

- *Who influences that audience?* Judging by the inordinate amount of public relations resources devoted to media relations, it seems that most PR people assume that the media have the greatest influence over their target audience. Nonetheless, in some cases the greatest influencer may be a member of the clergy, a politician, or a pop star. Understanding what motivates and influences your audience and who represents the most credible means for providing information and understanding is a great advantage. Even if your PR resources are devoted mostly to the media,

**Exhibit 2.1. Eleven Questions You Must
Ask Before Starting a Public Relations Program, Cont'd.**

having credible and engaging voices speaking for you and having a connection with opinion leaders is a great asset. The best way to discover
who influences your audience is to ask audience members themselves.
Qualitative research like focus groups and quantitative research like
surveys, both discussed in Chapter Three, are the preferred means of
determination.

- *Which media do your target audience read, watch, or listen to?* Once the target audience is identified, a media relations initiative focused on the select
media with the highest penetration among the target audience is made
more focused and efficient. Most PR media planning is based on intuition
and whichever journalists happen to be listed in your Rolodex file. The
world of advertising offers some better ways to approach media prioritization, which are rarely applied in public relations. These alternative
approaches are discussed in Chapter Three.

- *Who are your internal audiences?* Most public relations programs are externally focused on customers, on journalists, or on other opinion leaders.
Advance thinking about your internal audiences, however, can make or
break a PR plan. Consider the current environment in most workplaces
and you'll realize that among employees, one of the most trusted sources
of information about their own company is the media. So while communicating externally, consider the impact on your internal audiences. Further-
more, the organization's workforce is one of its primary customer-facing
elements. Well-informed employees, people who cheerfully and routinely
convey the organization's positivism among other employees, neighbors,
and customers, are among the organization's—and PR's—most powerful
assets.

- *Who are your internal clients?* Customers, professional colleagues, employees, opinion leaders, and journalists are all important, but the one who
determines the success or failure of your public relations program is the
"internal client," the executive who provides the funding. Knowing who
your internal clients are may be elementary, but understanding their perceptions and preferences for PR activities and outcomes can be difficult:
not knowing how your underwriters feel about your plans up front is risky
and dangerous—and just plain dumb. It is absolutely essential today to
know how your internal client feels about PR and to understand (and get
clear agreement on) the measures by which your PR success will be evaluated. Chapter Three introduces the Executive Audit, a simple survey
designed to reveal the often secret value systems at work in the minds
of internal clients.

Conclusion

In a sense, the challenges facing public relations are an affirmation of what it can accomplish. Rather than being justly ignored, PR has earned the right to be challenged in the same ways as other visible areas within the organization. PR has earned the right to be held as accountable as the sales force; PR has achieved sufficient status for its performance to be rated against the metrics that drive business; PR is a profession that deserves an educational substructure through which it will produce the talent of the future.

Questions Every PR Investment Decision Maker Should Ask

- Is our approach to marketing conventional or unconventional? Are we open to new and unconventional marketing thinking? Is PR in the mix?

- Have we explored how media relations–driven public relations can be an inexpensive means by which meaningful business results can be achieved?

- Do we sufficiently understand the new media landscape, including blogs, wikis, podcasts, and the rest? How do we put them to use on our behalf?

- How do we foster the professional development of our marketing and PR people? Have we created a culture that promotes interactive learning for more fully integrated marketing and communications thinking?

Part Two

USING RESEARCH
TO STRENGTHEN
PUBLIC RELATIONS

3

Measuring Public Relations Programming

Senior executives have begun to demand a measurable return on their investment in PR. Unfortunately, many PR professionals are unprepared to respond, and so we at Delahaye often hear things like, "For years, we've needed to more scientifically plan and measure our public relations . . . and I want to. Our executives are beginning to require it. But what is the best way to proceed? Will the results prove the value of PR? And what if the research shows that PR *isn't* performing?"

If these questions resemble your own, look at it this way: without the proper research-based underpinnings, you may never fully comprehend the extent of your accomplishments in a way that will allow you to reinforce and merchandise your success. And without a measurable, systematic approach to public relations objectives-setting, strategy development, and evaluation, you may never know enough about your performance to introduce improvements when needed. And finally, without a scientific approach to cataloguing, understanding, and applying what you learn to future endeavors, success will be fleeting rather than sustainable, and failures are bound to be repeated. The inevitable, unfortunate outcome of such an indeterminate state is that, while you're in it, the world accelerates without you.

So much can be gained when the rigor of science is married to the art of public relations: meaningful and positive business outcomes, market supremacy, and professional advancement. Companies that dominate their world because they understand and master their environment generate higher profits, attract and keep the best employees, and enjoy other forms of overall business success. The world's most admired companies didn't earn their reputations without carefully studying themselves in the mirror and then acting on what they saw—the ugly as well as the sublime. The only passage out of uncertainty is a direct one through which action leads to knowledge, and knowledge and understanding lead to success.

Those companies and public relations professionals who enjoy the benefits of PR research and evaluation begin by embracing the process fully: they relish their victories because their wins are validated and can be merchandized more credibly to those who fund PR programs. They also understand that uncovering shortfalls is a natural result of the process, especially in the beginning, but at least such shortfalls can be isolated and corrected. As a result, these well-informed practitioners lead with confidence and certainty.

The Science of PR

Traditional public relations is rooted in the social sciences. Edward Bernays, often cited as the "father of public relations" (and a nephew of Sigmund Freud), pioneered PR's use of psychology and other social sciences to design campaigns of public persuasion. He called this scientific opinion-molding technique the "engineering of consent," and described the PR counselor as a "practicing social scientist" whose "competence is like that of the industrial engineer, the management engineer, or the investment counselor in their respective fields." To assist clients, PR counselors used "understanding of the behavioral sciences and applying them—sociology, social psychology, anthropology, history, etc." Under this definition, research and evaluation are primary facets of PR.

The International Association of Business Communicators (IABC), like other professional communication societies, emphasizes research and measurement in its credo and mission statement. It defines itself as an organization whose mission it is to help members

- Make business sense of communication
- Think strategically about communication
- Measure and clarify the value of communication
- Build better relationships with stakeholders

As part of its definition of public relations, the Public Relations Society of America describes PR in these terms:

As a management function, public relations encompasses the following:

- Anticipating, analyzing and interpreting public opinion, attitudes, and issues that might impact, for good or ill, the operations and plans of the organization.
- Counseling management at all levels in the organization with regard to policy decisions, courses of action, and communications, taking into account their public ramifications and the organization's social or citizenship responsibilities.
- Researching, conducting, and evaluating, on a continuing basis, programs of action and communication to achieve the informed public understanding necessary to success of an organization's aims. These may include marketing, financial, fund raising, employee, community or government relations, and other programs.
- Planning and implementing the organization's efforts to influence or change public policy. Setting objectives, planning, budgeting, recruiting and training staff, developing facilities—in short, managing the resources needed to perform all of the above.

The examples of Bernays, the IABC, and the PRSA would suggest that scientific measurement is a critical component of public relations. Unfortunately, as PR is routinely practiced, the formal process of research and measurement comes as an afterthought.

According to the 2005 edition of the "Annual Corporate Survey" conducted by *PRWeek* (www.prweek.com), one of the most widely read and respected among the PR journals, less than 2 percent of the average PR budget goes toward research and evaluation. Moreover, what respondents regard as research and evaluation isn't quite clear; they could be thinking of methods that are statistically reliable and meaningful—or of piles of press clippings. (While tabulating clips is useful for tracking publicity, it does not, in and of itself, qualify as research and evaluation.)

Given the magnitude of the opportunities and the challenges being faced by business today, there has to be a better way. The good news is that alternatives are within the reach of almost every PR person: they can just as often be simple as sophisticated and economical just as often as expensive. Whether simple or sophisticated, research comes in a variety of forms. The savvy PR person will have at least a basic understanding of different types of research and the sorts of information the different forms of research can provide.

What You Need to Know About PR Research

Three forms of research should be considered in public relations: *primary research*, which centers on conducting original studies and developing new data; *secondary research*, which is based on the mining of preexisting data and information; and *statistical modeling*, which seeks to create some greater learning through the unified statistical analysis of disparate sources of data, both primary and secondary.

Primary research usually involves a process of questioning respondents in search of greater insight. The type of primary research that yields objective, statistically based results is known as *quantitative* research, most frequently conducted in the form of a *survey*. When done properly, quantitative research yields findings that can be projected to a larger population. Quantitative researchers gather data in a variety of ways, but the most common methods include telephone, Web site, mail, and e-mail surveys, each of which offers distinct advantages and disadvantages in terms of speed, cost, flexibility, and levels of audience participation.

The other form of primary research is known as *qualitative* research, most commonly conducted in the form of *focus groups*. Focus groups consist of a dozen people or so who are encouraged under the direction of a facilitator to share opinions, frustrations, likes, and dislikes relating to the subject under discussion. Focus groups are very useful for generating ideas and guidance but their results cannot be projected upon a larger population. For this reason, focus groups are often misused when organizations in search of some quick, inexpensive feedback substitute focus group results for quantitative research. When properly used, qualitative research is staged as a precursor to quantitative research so that the survey can be that much more effective.

Statistical modeling is a process used in marketing and public relations analysis to mathematically explain historical results and predict future outcomes. These analyses focus on probabilities and trends based on a number of variable factors that are likely to influence future behavior or results. In marketing, for example, a customer's gender, age, and purchase history might predict the likelihood of a future sale. To create a predictive model, data are collected for the relevant predictors, a statistical model is formulated, predictions are made, and the model is validated (or revised) as additional data become available. In public relations, statistical models can be used to uncover the effect of PR and its interaction with other marketing and communication agents, as well as such external factors as the weather and population, on behavioral outcomes. When models of this type are applied to sales, they are known as "marketing mix models" and they seek to provide insight into what drives purchasing behavior.

Research Tools for Effective
Public Relations Measurement

While public relations can employ an array of research applications, three tools for scientific measurement and evaluation are fundamental:

- Surveys
- News content analysis
- Statistical modeling

Survey Research

Surveys are a quantified assessment of the attitudes of a person or of a group toward a subject, developed as a result of earlier influences. Most survey research involves questioning a representative sample of individuals. Very carefully designed questionnaires, usually administered in a structured manner, can uncover attitudes, needs, or preferences.

Survey Design. It seems that whenever a survey is being considered, everyone jumps right to working up the questions, the fun and exciting part. It's fast and easy to throw around interesting ideas, but the hard part—and the part that will determine whether or not the survey, the objectives-setting, and even the entire program, for that matter, are a success—is the survey design. The wording, the order, the choice of open-ended and closed questions do a great deal to determine whether the survey will provide the results you're seeking. Given the importance of survey design, it's best to work with experienced survey researchers.

Sample Selection. The *sample* is another term for "the people you invite to participate in your survey." It is almost always impractical to speak with everyone in your target audience, so it's fortunate that you need to interview only a relatively small representation of the more general population. By *representation*, we mean that the people who are interviewed should mirror the makeup of your target audience. One of the reasons why presidential polling is so accurate is that the people who are polled match the general makeup of the U.S. population. Similarly, your survey sample needs to accurately match your program's target audience in such areas as age, gender, income, purchasing history, political affiliation, and possibly dozens of other factors. Broad-based sample profiles, such as "men aged twenty-one to forty-five," are almost meaningless since they are so inclusive as to make your results difficult to apply. To be useful and meaningful, the samples are often subdivided into smaller representative segments. To be valid, each segment ought to feature no fewer than three hundred interviews but need not be greater than a thousand, depending on the total population being considered, the number of slices of the data, your budget, and so on. The key is how many people are within each segment, not the overall number of interviews.

Format. A survey can be conducted on a variety of platforms including face-to-face and telephone interviews (using a professional interviewer), mail, e-mail, and the Web. Some are fast, others are relatively inexpensive, still others are especially suitable for a given situation. In our experience, face-to-face interviews allow for the highest level of interaction and the most thoughtful exchange but they are also the most expensive and time-consuming, and since this form of interviewing is the most intrusive form of data collection, one might find interviewees reluctant to participate. Mail, e-mail, and Web data-collection techniques are the fastest and least expensive but they also tend to attract only the bored or the polarized: if people have nothing better to do, or if they love or hate the subject matter, they may be motivated to participate. For the indifferent majority, you may have to provide an incentive to attract a necessary volume of responses. We find that telephone interviews are the most attractive middle ground: less expensive and less intrusive than in-person interviews but still allowing for interaction and follow-up questions.

Cost. Research is often viewed as something too expensive and too sophisticated for most public relations programs, but many low- or no-cost research services can be found. Given the importance of the objectives-setting stage (as discussed in Chapter Four) and what can be learned to protect future investments, it would be wise to spend a bit at the beginning of the program rather than waste time and money on strategies and tactics that have little chance for success. A lot of what can be gained in a PR objectives-setting survey can be accomplished in conjunction with other market research studies under way within your organization. Even though deployed for other marketing and communication endeavors, they provide ways to share costs with other interested departments.

One type of cost-effective attitudinal survey is called an *omnibus*. Omnibus surveys are funded by several participants, each of whom pays to ask a limited number of questions among a particular target group. The fee is thereby distributed among a group of interested parties (rather than each having to shoulder the entire cost of an independent survey). Omnibus surveys are helpful if you need to control costs and assemble information quickly. The order of questions, however, is a major downside to using omnibuses since you can't control or even know where your questions will appear within the list of questions. This is made worse if the overall intent is to conduct tracking studies, since the question context is likely to be very different each time the omnibus is repeated.

We've heard of some extraordinarily successful surveys being undertaken at universities, where professors are eager to find real-world opportunities for their students (and also subsidies for the research effort). Another low-cost alternative are Web-based survey tools like Survey Monkey, which are within the reach of almost every PR budget and can be used in-house with very little training.

Using Surveys

Although there are many types of surveys, three are simple enough to begin using today:

- *The Executive Audit:* A survey instrument for building consensus among those who fund or influence PR programs. See sample questionnaire in Appendix 1.
- *The Media Demographic Audit:* A database of media habits and lifestyle characteristics based on the results of a syndicated survey. See sample report in Appendix 2.
- *The Journalist Audit:* A survey among key journalists to uncover the means to improve media relationships. See sample questionnaire in Appendix 3.

The Executive Audit: Proving Value Through Greater Understanding.   The first requirement for proving value in terms of generating a "return on expectation" is met through the application of an Executive Audit—a survey of the senior executives who underwrite PR programs. Some executives know what is reasonable and achievable through the use of PR while others don't, but the audit is a clean-slate approach to uncovering what PR underwriters do know and what they seek from public relations—for example, "delivering key messages to target media" or "increased awareness" or even "increased sales"—matched with the executives' assessment of current PR performance. The Executive Audit, a form of qualitative research, is usually done via a brief telephone survey of internal public relations clients who have a primary impact on PR strategy, goal setting, and evaluation.

The Executive Audit measures the attitudes, preferences, needs, and expectations of top management when working with their public relations departments. These interviews gather information directly from executives about

- Their attitudes, preferences, needs, and expectations for your public relations effort in terms of

  Goals and objectives of the organization and how they relate to public relations and corporate communication

  Professional attributes (good writing, media skills, and so on)

  Activities and tactics (media relations, strategic PR guidance, and so on)

  Achievement of client and company-wide objectives

  Media considered most credible, most important

  Messages considered most credible, most compelling

- The standards by which they measure public relations effectiveness (and what drives success in the opinion of this key audience)

- The extent to which public relations now satisfies these preferences, needs, and expectations

Executive Audits also set the stage for ongoing dialogue in terms that are meaningful, educational, and consensus building. They provide the feedback needed by public relations professionals to continually improve departmental and personal performance in meeting the needs of key executives. Delahaye conducts hundreds of executive interviews each year and the results indicate that PR investors have a good understanding of what measures are reasonable, meaningful, and feasible. Interestingly, executive assessments of current PR practices indicate that public relations departments tend to overdeliver on what PR underwriters value least (a high volume of press clippings), while underdelivering on what they value most (raising awareness and delivering key messages to target media). Once these preferences and assessments are discussed and understood, more formal standards may be established against which value can be clearly demonstrated.

An example of how an Executive Audit can work was demonstrated in the case of a consumer packaged goods company whose

PR department labored for weeks to produce fancy clip books, with press cuttings individually mounted on colored paper and enclosed in leather-bound covers. They were beautiful, but executives couldn't have cared less. The audit results revealed what mattered: not just the volume of clips but the quality of coverage generated from target media. From that time forward, the company devoted a greater share of its resources on just "A-list" media, which were also identified by the executives and then verified using the Media Demographic Audit (discussed in the next section). Executives gained a more meaningful gauge of PR performance, and the PR department saved tens of thousands of dollars by *not* targeting and tracking secondary, ineffectual media outlets.

The Media Demographic Audit. One of the most critical steps in any marketing and communication endeavor is that of *targeting,* the process of identifying and reaching the audience considered to be the optimal subject of your communication and marketing effort. What we call the Media Demographic Audit is a form of secondary research that provides detailed analysis of national and local consumer print, broadcast, and Internet (as well as trade and consumer) media viewership, listenership, and readership. Circulation tabulations are a simple and easily understood measure of media reach, but this audit provides detailed information regarding *targeted audience reach:*

- Demographics, geographics, and psychographics
- Products and services owned and planning to purchase (including brand names)
- Leisure activities
- Media involvement

The Media Demographic Audit is used by PR professionals to manage their media relations plan more strategically in terms of targeting, positioning, and return on investment.

Since the Media Demographic Audit develops detailed information about *your* target audience—who they are; what they own; what they do; and the media they read, watch, and listen to—you can make the most of your limited public relations resources by targeting only the most productive print, broadcast, and Internet media.

The audit goes beyond conventional PR wisdom to provide *target customer–driven* planning and evaluation. For example, a luxury car manufacturer may use the audit to target luxury car owners—but only those expressing intent to purchase a new luxury car within the next twelve months. The car manufacturer can target by a number of other criteria, too: for example, by brand, by price range, by preference for domestic or import, and by the timing of their intended purchase. Further refinement comes by indexing versus age, income, and other brackets. Criteria such as these are entered into the demographics database to uncover just those media whose target audience fits the description, and out comes a list identifying the best fits.

The Journalist Audit.   The Journalist Audit, a form of qualitative research, is a brief telephone survey of journalists at media that matter who have a primary impact on the success of your public relations programs. The survey solicits feedback designed to help you continually improve the quality and quantity of your media coverage.

The Journalist Audit measures the attitudes, preferences, needs, and expectations key journalists have for working with public relations departments. The Journalist Audit is used to achieve a number of purposes:

- To accurately assess journalists' attitudes, preferences, needs, and expectations for your public relations effort in terms of
    Professional attributes (responsive, accessible, and so on)
    Activities and tactics (pitch calls, releases, events)

Which of your competitors are best at PR, what they do that makes them best, and how you compare to the best on a variety of attributes

- To help define the standards by which public relations effectiveness is measured (and what drives success in the opinion of this key audience)

- To determine the extent to which your public relations efforts now satisfy these preferences, needs, and expectations compared to your competitors' efforts

- To set the stage for continual improvement as evidenced in how the journalists treat your organization editorially and how your organization performs in the next annual Journalist Audit

Journalists are surprisingly outspoken when it comes to providing guidance to PR departments. In one example, journalists told us that our client (whom we had not identified as the sponsor of our study) was generally unresponsive and inaccessible for interview requests. Once our client's PR department learned that as a result of the distance created between company and journalist, the company's volume and quality of news coverage was less than its competitors enjoyed, it changed its ways and made sure that the company's senior executives were always available for comment.

Beyond Surveys: Content Analysis

One particularly popular application of media relations–based PR research is news content analysis, a method for tracking how the activities of a PR program—press conferences, special events, press releases, speeches—actually affect stories in the media. According to the indispensable *Webster's New World Dictionary of Media and Communications* (written by Richard Weiner—no relation but highly esteemed), "News content analyses are a research technique of studying media in order to systematically and objectively identify the characteristics of the messages."

Content analysis begins with gathering print, broadcast, and Internet content through the use of a media monitoring service like Romeike in the United Kingdom, Observer in the Nordic regions, Argus in Germany, Bowden's in Canada, or Bacon's in the United States; a news retrieval database like Lexis-Nexis or Factiva; an Internet-based monitoring service like Moreover or Cyberalert; or by just combing the Web or hard-copy media yourself. The content, in the form of newspaper and magazine articles, radio and television coverage, and Internet news, discussion groups, and blogs, contains a variety of themes and messages that need to be coded for references to a particular organization or an idea. Once coded, the resulting data are analyzed to determine trends and opinions. For example, in the case of a pharmaceutical company's new drug release, PR researchers scan consumer and trade press clippings, broadcast transcripts, and online health discussion groups for references to a campaign in which the new drug is promoted as being *safe*, *fast-acting*, and *reasonably priced*. They catalogue and analyze the intended positive references—along with any unintended negative references, say, to the company's recent poor track record with FDA approvals or the company's financial performance—to determine trends and perceptions relevant to that particular drug and its manufacturer.

In practical terms and in its most common form, content analysis is used as a means to report on the volume and quality of news coverage during a specified time period. In the pharmaceutical example, the time periods may reflect the FDA process: "pre-approval," "approval," and "post-approval." The resulting data are presented on a monthly, quarterly, or annual basis to reflect not just the individual campaign but also the larger context of all campaigns and all company and brand news. Typically, these reports include information such as the name of the publication or TV program, the date the story appeared, and the circulation or audience, along

with a register of the messages contained in the story and the overall tone of the story. Like all the research tools discussed in this
chapter, the content analysis is used *to prove* and *to improve* the perceived value of PR by demonstrating current value and providing
guidance for future efforts.

Content analysis at its most basic level involves tabulating stories in the media; more sophisticated levels track tone, assess specific messages, analyze results against competitors' efforts, and at
their most sophisticated, measure PR's impact on behavior.

Stage One: Media Tabulations. As shown in Figure 3.1, even
simple forms of news content analysis can provide useful insight.
This example uses a popular spreadsheet program to create charts
and graphs that show simple measures such as frequency (clip volume) and reach (circulation and audience) data. When tracked
from one quarter to the next over time, they provide an indication
of the direction of the PR program in terms of the number of stories
generated and the number of people who had an opportunity to
read, watch, or hear what was being communicated.

Figure 3.1. Volume of Coverage (Frequency) by Number of News Items.

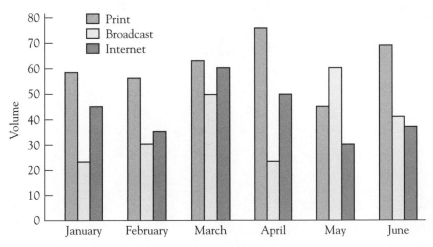

Simple tracking also allows for the same results to be viewed in a variety of ways. Table 3.1 illustrates a listing of the most receptive media outlets for a particular client.

As simple as this sort of table may seem, the user can see at a glance if the program is trending up or down from month to month, and might also be able to attach the timing of certain outputs to the corresponding results. If the second quarter saw an increase of almost 100 percent over the first, was there a publicity campaign or a special event under way during that period? Another simple measure that you can accomplish in-house and on your own is tracking for media type. In the example shown in Figure 3.2, the pie chart

Table 3.1. Year-to-Date Top Media.

Media	Frequency	Percentage Versus Prior Year	Number Versus Prior Year
Chicago Tribune	111	+19	+64
Investor Business Journal	99	+13	+59
Financial Times	88	+18	+42
Australian Financial Review	77	+16	+39
Newsbytes	66	+4	+27

Figure 3.2. Coverage by Medium.

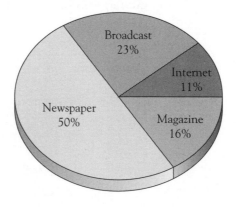

indicates that almost 50 percent of the news generated on this particular subject came from daily newspapers. If newspapers were the focus of this campaign, it would indicate that the plan worked as it was designed to work. However, if most of the campaign's resources were directed toward magazines, the same chart signals that it would be useful to review and adjust the allocation.

This sort of simple media analysis is well within reach of anyone in PR who has access to Microsoft Excel or any other spreadsheet and charting software. All it takes is to create a spreadsheet with column headings such as *date of coverage*, *circulation*, and *media type*.

Stage Two: Measuring Tone. Up to now, examples such as *media tabulations* have focused more on the *quantity* of coverage than on its *quality*. As a result, it is not yet feasible to say whether the program was successful or not. The first step toward measuring the quality of coverage is to introduce the assessment of *tone*. Tone should be applied toward individual messages rather than the entire story. It can be measured by simply using a three-point *positive-neutral-negative* scale, but we suggest a five-point scale since most themes are neither totally positive nor totally negative. The five-point scale offers a higher level of granularity, using a scale ranging from *totally negative* (−2) to *somewhat negative* (−1) to *neutral* (0) to *somewhat positive* (+1) to *totally positive* (+2). Figure 3.3 illustrates a program that's enjoying a great deal of success: 91 percent of the coverage was either neutral or positive, which indicates an extraordinary degree of control. Whereas most programs wind up mirroring a traditional bell curve, with equal amounts of news coverage at both "Very Positive" and "Very Negative," in this case 31 percent is "Very Positive" and only 5 percent is "Very Negative." An executive who knows just a little about public relations can appreciate the performance of this program.

The individual message scores are then aggregated to determine the "favorability" of a story, again using a scale of −2 to +2. At this stage, it becomes clear whether the high volume of widely seen coverage is a good thing or a bad thing: O. J. Simpson continues to

Figure 3.3. Tone of Coverage.

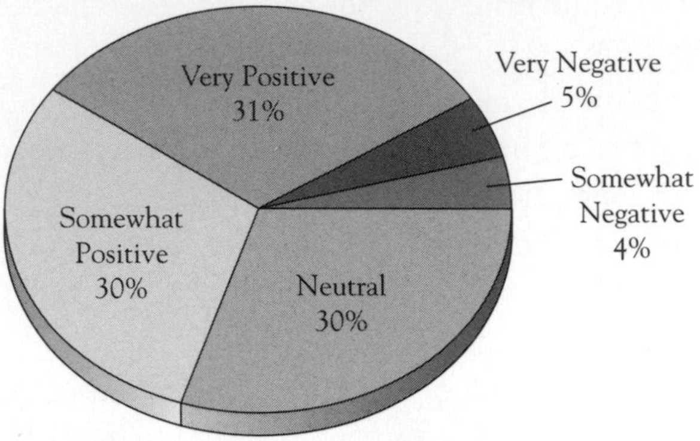

generate news coverage but it isn't the type of visibility to which anyone would aspire.

Stage Three: Message Tracking. A still more advanced level of analysis tracks the presence and the tone of individual messages. Message tracking is essential for planning for success and evaluating results as it provides a level of granularity for managing for continual improvement. For example, Delahaye used survey research to develop a key message list on behalf of the domestic pharmaceutical division of a Fortune 100 company. The company had licensed a heart medication that was relatively late to market. The research showed that the unique messaging opportunity for the drug was "just as safe and effective as other heart medications but for much lower cost." The message tracking performed as part of our content analysis showed that the messaging appeared often and that it was positively represented. The directive to this client was keep up the good work. Other studies have revealed underperforming messages that required refinement.

In the example in Figure 3.4, it is easy to see the extent to which the organization's key messages are being delivered as well as the tone of the messages delivered. The five basic message types described on the bars might be used for any organization, large or

Figure 3.4. Key Messages.

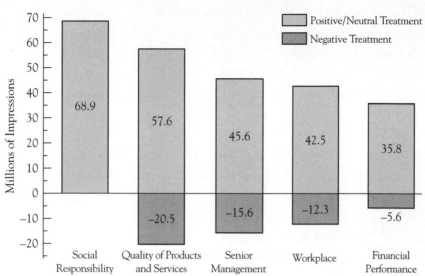

small, for-profit and nonprofit. At Delahaye, we call these five the "Core Messages" for that reason. Core Messages are the umbrella under which the supporting messages of a business entity would communicate or generate specific information or responses. And if you track competitors as you track your own organization, Core Messages allow you to make apples-to-apples comparisons. For example, there was the well-known gasoline retailer (in other words, branded gas stations) for whom we tracked "pay at the pump" to represent how people can pump their own gas. The client outperformed all competitors on that message, but it wasn't until later that it was learned that "pay at the pump" is a copyrighted slogan that applied to only one brand of gasoline. A core message like "quality of products and services" would have allowed for a more direct comparison at the 30,000-foot level, and supporting messages like "pump your own gas" could have isolated that particular attribute from others.

Of the five messages shown, some seem to be working according to plan, while others seem to warrant improvement. For example,

Social Responsibility themes are appearing most frequently and there are only positive mentions. If this is a key message for this campaign, then the strategy is working. If, on the other hand, *Quality of Products and Services* is the key theme for this campaign, there's cause for concern: a high volume of coverage but an unusually high ratio of negative-to-positive, which would suggest that corrective action might be necessary.

Although this level of message analysis can be done in-house, it requires a degree of involvement and objectivity that most organizations find difficult to undertake. Nonetheless, at this level it becomes easier to see where the possibilities for truly strategic, research-based public relations can be realized.

Stage Four: Competitive Tracking. To take the content analysis to another level, one may add competitors to the mix. This is a point at which complexity and cost may become considerations, so I recommend two ways to reduce the volume of clips and the time required to analyze them. First, identify the media that matter— that is, rather than tracking every publication and TV show, select only those known to be most important (as mentioned in Exhibit 2.1, "Eleven Questions You Must Ask Before Starting a Public Relations Program") or those with the highest penetration among the target audience. Second, identify the competitors most worth tracking, and that usually reduces the list to two or three: your company, the market-share leader (if it isn't you), and the market innovator, or the company who may be responsible for changing the landscape of your category, as in Figure 3.5. An example among airlines might be American, United, and JetBlue, representing two traditional leaders and the upstart innovator.

As the complexity increases, so does the capacity of the analysis to drive learning and insight. At this point, a process known as *message engineering* becomes possible. The theory is that if a message is important, frequently seen, and positive, then all you need to do is reinforce the effort. If a message is important, frequently seen, and negative, then you have a situation you need to fix.

Figure 3.5. Competitive Brand Message Chart.

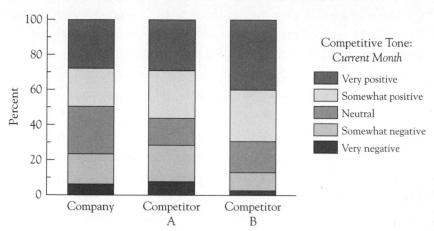

Stage Five: The Public Relations Gross Rating Point. For years, there has been a growing desire to represent media coverage as something more than just hits. The understanding among those people who fund PR programs is that clippings are just an incremental goal toward something more meaningful, such as *awareness, understanding, preference,* and *behavior.* With such measures available to marketers, public relations can be more easily integrated with and compared to other forms of marketing and communication.

Any discussion of PR's relationship and interaction with other forms of marketing must begin with an understanding of how various forms of marketing work. Public relations, as discussed in Chapter Two, is only "semi-controllable," at best. Output activities are undertaken and they make the news or not, depending on the editor's judgment. Advertising and direct marketing, on the other hand, are 100 percent controllable since you pay a specific price that gives you specific control of frequency, reach, and positioning.

In managing their controllable form of marketing communication, advertisers use copy and advertising testing (through qualitative and quantitative research discussed earlier) to make sure that the ads they eventually run will be compelling, involving, and persuasive to the mass market. Once the visuals and content are finalized, advertisers plan and evaluate their ad spend using an industry measure known as a *Gross Rating Point* (GRP), which represents the *reach* (circulation and audience) and the *frequency* (the number of times an ad runs) of the campaign. Since the communication is controlled, the only variance left to consider is how many GRPs the campaign will put against its level of spending in a particular time frame and in a given market.

Since public relations is only semi-controllable, copy and advertising testing in their traditional forms do not apply—you can't know in advance if the magazine will use the product photograph or if the TV program will feature the product name in the lead story. As a result, a new form of measurement had to be created. This measure would have to represent PR's unique role accurately in the marketing mix and foster the true integration of PR with other forms of marketing and communication—a "PR-GRP"—and this is precisely what we did. Here's the story:

Creating PR's GRP: The Impact Score and Net Effect. The key consideration for creating a PR-GRP was the degree to which PR can and cannot be controlled. The PR-GRP not only had to represent reach and frequency, as in advertising's GRP, it also had to represent the quality or impact of news coverage. And finally, again reflecting PR's semi-controllable nature, the PR-GRP could only be applied *after* a story appeared (but it had to be useful as a tool by which story quality could be managed going forward).

The Impact Score is PR's GRP: the first distilled measure for the purposes of planning and evaluating media activity. It was known from the beginning that the formula would have to include factors something like these: Frequency × Reach × Quality. The challenge became, How does one define *quality?* And then, How does one distill these three measures into a single number?

The initial research into creating the Impact Score had three objectives:

- To identify the attributes that denote quality in media coverage
- To assess their relative weight in influencing the likelihood that someone would first notice and then remember the news coverage (awareness and recall)
- To combine these factors into an easy-to-use, integrated marketing performance measure

For the first phase of the analysis, we focused on print media—although Impact Score has since been extended to broadcast and Web-based media. We began by creating a list of attributes thought to indicate quality in a news story. The list contained more than forty possibilities; one, for example, tracked dominance within coverage from "a story reporting news exclusively about one company" to "a roundup story mentioning several companies."

A representative sample of coverage was gathered from a variety of news sources. Stories were selected and then coded by expert media analysts. Some attributes were rated on a scale of 1 to 5 with 1 being the lowest value and 5 being the highest, where, for example, a 1 would indicate "a roundup story mentioning several companies" and a 5 "a story reporting news exclusively about one company." Other attributes were binary, in that the attribute was either present or not, such as the presence or absence of a visual (photo or graphic, for example) representing the company. Each of the attributes was scored for each of the articles. The tone of the article (the editorial attitude conveyed toward the company) was also assessed, as it would be applied as an overall factor by which the attributes would be multiplied, so that a 5, representing "an exclusive story with a photo" in a *positive* article was just as good as a 5 in a *negative* article would be bad. In this way, a content analysis of each of the news stories was completed using each of the forty attributes.

The second phase was designed to reveal the extent to which each of the forty attributes under consideration actually drove awareness and recall among a representative group of a thousand people. Copies of each article were distributed in a controlled environment and the participants were asked first to read each news item and then (later) asked the extent to which they remembered specific stories and story themes. After the data collection and analysis were complete, certain stories emerged as the most memorable, and these stories each contained common story attributes that turned out to be the key drivers of awareness and recall. These story attributes (now called *Prominence*) form the basis for Delahaye's Impact Score measure of media performance.

While the precise formula is proprietary, the Prominence factors (summarized in Exhibit 3.1) include the following:

- *News item placement:* The front page, front cover, or television news intro is the most desirable spot within the publication or the program (using a scale of 1–2: you're either there or you're not).
- *Headline:* The headline in a print story (or the lead intro in a TV newscast) is the most noticeable and most memorable part of a particular news item (using a 1–2 scale: you're either in the headline or lead or you're not).
- *Initial mention:* The location of the first mention of your organization or brand, with the most powerful placement being at the beginning of the news item (where a 1 represents the initial mention occurring at the end of the story and a 5 representing the initial mention right at the beginning).
- *Extent of mention:* The size of the news item, where the larger, longer, or bigger the better (where a 1 represents a tiny mention and a 5 represents a large feature).
- *Dominance:* The degree to which the story is about you or about competitors on a scale of 1–5 (where a 1 indicates that your media mention is shared with many others, and where a 5 means that the story represents only one organization).
- *Visuals:* The appearance of photographs and other visuals on a scale of 1–2 (there either is a visual or there isn't one).

Exhibit 3.1. The Impact Score.

- Reach
- Frequency
- Impact
    - Front page or cover
    - Headline or lead
    - Initial mention
    - Extent of mention
    - Dominance
    - Visuals
- Presence of Key Messages
- Tone

The Impact Score is a composite of Prominence and Tone that becomes a quality score on a scale of +100 percent to –100 percent (Tone determines whether the score is a *positive* or *negative* number). Prominence is a research-based estimation of the likelihood that someone will be exposed to and remember news about a company. Prominence factors are weighted based on their relative contribution to news item quality.

The performance of each element within the Impact Score is transparent and can be managed for continual improvement. As shown in Table 3.2, the company being analyzed generates a very high percentage of positive coverage, but very few of the stories include a visual or a graphic. Graphics and visuals are powerful drivers of recall and awareness, and this company should consider introducing more visuals in its corporate storytelling. All told, a newspaper story in which you are mentioned on the front page, in the headline, with visuals, where the story is all about you and positive is about as good as it gets: when the same attributes are mirrored but the story is negative (again, think of Enron), you've got problems. It is much better for your negative news to be contained in a small, inconspicuous industry roundup story buried in the back pages.

Table 3.2. Competitive Impact Score Factor Illustration.

Factors	Company		Competitor A		Competitor B	
	Frequency	Percent of Total Clips	Frequency	Percent of Total Clips	Frequency	Percent of Total Clips
Front Page	9	3	4	3	6	2
Headline	70	21	11	7	79	20
Exclusive Mention	226	58	97	59	204	47
Significant Mention	35	9	16	10	48	11
Lead Mention	158	40	55	34	158	37
Visual or Graphic	2	1	4	3	6	2
Very or Somewhat Positive Tone	347	89	149	91	365	85

The Impact Score is continually and uniquely validated during dozens of rigorous statistical analyses each year, and has been shown to be a reliable and consistent distilled score for representing PR's presence within the marketing mix. What is more, it has been used to demonstrate PR's ability to drive meaningful business outcomes such as awareness and behavior. While the actual weighting is a trade secret, it is important that PR people all know that what they have always believed to be true has been quantified: public relations can deliver incremental sales and profits to an organization, and the Impact Score unlocks the possibilities of proving it.

"Net Effect" is the result of the Reach of an individual news item multiplied by its Impact Score. Results are combined to determine an overall Net Effect for a specific period of time, or surrounding a particular issue or event. Net Effect can be *positive* or *negative*. In every case in which the Impact Score and Net Effect have been applied in either marketing mix models or Six Sigma situations (detailed in Chapter Seven), the result has been statistically reliable correlations tying PR to better performance, whether performance is measured in sales, productivity, or efficiency.

Marketing Mix Modeling

Marketing mix modeling is an analysis that draws data from disparate sources and applies advanced statistical analysis to provide insight into the efficiency and effectiveness of ongoing marketing programs (see Figure 3.6). Using traditional databases, like sales, advertising Gross Rating Points, or content analysis, researchers merge the data to create more complete views of the marketplace and to estimate the impact on sales of advertising, PR, pricing, merchandising, competitive activity, seasonality, and other factors. Given an understanding of what drives sales, it becomes possible to explain past results and influence future sales. The importance of knowing in advance what drives sales promises a revolution in the marketing and communications world.

Figure 3.6. Marketing Mix Modeling Process.

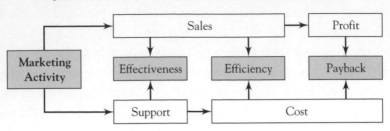

As new approaches and more powerful technologies become available, PR's capacity to properly assess and accurately forecast marketing performance has never been greater. It is in this new environment that the die is being cast: management is beginning to use two words—*prove it*—and soon you may have no choice but to do so.

To be sure, the need for and the increased access to marketing intelligence hasn't led to a sea change for marketers *yet*. Television advertising, promotions, and direct marketing continue to command significant spending, and their need to demonstrate and generate a positive ROI is scaled to the level of investment. But the day is coming when each of these marketing functions will be judged on its ability to deliver *value;* those consuming the greatest resources will feel the most pressure first. On the basis of relative spending, public relations may seem like a lower priority. But in terms of ROI, public relations may be the most critical, because marketing mix modeling analyses have repeatedly demonstrated that PR delivers a superior ROI, and an investment in public relations often delivers a lift to other forms of marketing.

As a result, PR has the most to gain in this new environment. But to achieve some higher level of primacy, PR departments have to change the way they work. Success will be contingent upon PR's willingness to work in a more integrated fashion with other marketing agents, and to use proven research techniques to clearly demonstrate a positive and meaningful ROI. In this setting, marketing decisions will be based on what drives results rather than on outmoded ideas of "what we've always done"; public relations strategies based on empty goals such as "generate significant buzz" will get left by the wayside.

Companies whose names you'd recognize in categories as diverse as retail, automotive, telecom, consumer packaged goods, financial services, and motion pictures are feeding advanced news content analysis into sophisticated marketing mix models to make the PR-to-sales connection. In its own right, the content analysis gives PR people the feedback they need to do a better job in delivering a high quantity of quality media coverage. But when content analysis results are fed into a statistical model along with other marketing data to tweak out the relative power of PR, advertising, direct marketing, telemarketing, trade marketing, and the rest, the result is an ROI road map for decision making. Savvy companies apply what they learn by shifting their emphasis within the marketing mix to drive the optimal combination of marketing for sales. It won't be long before PR efforts (along with every other form of marketing) are planned on the basis of "what drives sales" rather than "what drives buzz"—and you'd better prepare for it.

Clearly, understanding the value and ROI of public relations holds huge promise for marketers in general and public relations professionals in particular. While the result of this type of analysis often brings with it increased budgets and staffing, it also has provided companies with opportunities to focus their precious marketing and communication resources on programs that deliver. The savings derived from cutting nonperforming programs allows for human and financial resources to be reallocated in ways that have helped PR departments voluntarily reduce budgets while generating even better results.

The Measurement Revolution Is Here

If it hasn't happened to you already, the day is soon coming when you will be asked to prove it. Public relations research and evaluation methods have reached a point where PR pros can feel confident—

not just in being able to respond but in taking the initiative to uncover new opportunities for savings, value, and positive ROI.

The PR measurement revolution is happening, and it's happening with you or without you. To join the revolution, PR professionals need to take several steps:

- Become acquainted with the science of public relations.
- Take charge rather than waiting.
- Embrace the challenge.
- Act now while others commit to beginning tomorrow.

It is a matter of becoming the master of your professional destiny, being fully awake, aware, and intelligent—in sum, being truly professional.

Questions Every PR Investment Decision Maker Should Ask

- Are we conducting solid, salient PR research?
- Are we mistaking qualitative research for quantitative?
- Does our PR department accurately understand the values of the organization? When was the last time we conducted an Executive Audit?
- Can we identify the markets with the highest concentration of our target audience? How about the media they read, watch, and listen to?
- How do journalists feel about us? When working on a tight deadline, whom do they call first? If it isn't us, why isn't it?
- Do we do more than clip counting when assessing the media's treatment of our company, our brands, and the issues we've prioritized?

- Are our marketing departments aligned? Are we using advanced statistical analyses to ensure that our marketing and communication resources are optimized? Do we know which agents deliver the best ROI? If so, have we shifted priorities in light of what we've learned?

- When it comes to the "PR measurement revolution," are we leaders, followers, or under the guillotine?

4

Setting Meaningful and Measurable Public Relations Objectives

For your PR efforts to realize their full potential, you need to start with a clean slate: no preset objectives, preconceived strategies, or predetermined outcomes. This clean-slate atmosphere provides a fresh start for reexamining the priorities of the organization, how they affect public relations, and what public relations can do to advance these priorities. It begins with a dispassionate look at past performance, conventional wisdom, and what has come before, from either within the organization or among its competitors: everything is up for grabs. It is a landscape ripe for new thinking in support of breakthrough opportunities and explosive growth.

Clean-slate public relations is a layering process that begins and ends with research: the progression begins with the research upon which objectives will be set and by which strategy can be developed. It continues with the creative interpretation of the initial research for the purposes of creating and delivering key messages to target audiences in a compelling and credible fashion. The sequence moves forward through program execution in a way that advanced research has pretested for success, and concludes with the research-based evaluation by which the PR program is assessed in terms of the extent to which it met or exceeded the original research-based objectives. But rather than working in a linear fashion, the process is cyclical, with each succeeding program being a bit more refined, more efficient, and more effective. This chapter and each of the three that follow focuses on a specific research element within the sequence.

While each component of this scientific approach is integral to the development, execution, and evaluation of successful public relations programs, it can be argued that the initial stage of objectives-setting research is the most important and certainly the most frequently overlooked: it is at once the foundation for the entire PR program and the skeleton around which strategy, execution, and evaluation are formed.

Why Setting Objectives for Public Relations Is Essential

Despite the truism that you need to know your destination in order to tell whether you've arrived, the vast majority of public relations programs do not begin with a clear and measurable objective. As a result, when it comes time to measure performance against objectives, few PR programs can prove the extent to which—or even if—they succeeded.

There are five simple reasons for setting clear and concise objectives in public relations:

- *Objectives create a structure for prioritizing action:* Once your aim is clear, so too becomes the sequence of actions required to achieve it.

- *Objectives reduce the potential for disputes before, during, and after the program:* Once everyone has agreed on the objective and the strategy by which you intend to meet or surpass the objective, the risk of disagreement is greatly minimized as everyone works with a single sense of understanding and purpose.

- *Objectives increase efficiency by concentrating resources where they will make a difference, thereby reducing waste and inefficiency:* A clear sense of purpose distills program tactics and focuses assets where they have the greatest impact.

- *Objectives help to form successful programs by focusing attention and action on those criteria by which the program will later be evaluated:* Good and proper objectives provide a clear line of sight. When they share an advanced understanding of the criteria for success, teams naturally work toward those areas that will yield the desired outcome.

- *Objectives set the stage for evaluation by allowing PR investment decision makers to determine if the PR program met or exceeded its original objectives:* Objectives work best when they are understood and acknowledged by those who are underwriting the investment. Once you set specific objectives and gain agreement in advance, there can be no doubt as to whether the program met or fell short of the desired outcome at the time of its conclusion. (Of course, there are some who view this type of vagueness as a plus. . . . But they're planning for failure before they get started.)

However compelling the reasons for setting clear, measurable objectives are, it is done too infrequently. The award programs sponsored by professional PR associations and trade publications reveal that a haphazard approach to setting objectives is widespread in the world of PR. Each year, professional communicators from corporations, nonprofits, PR agencies, and governments are invited to submit "best-in-class" PR programs for consideration to win the profession's most esteemed awards. The awards are considered an important distinction of accomplishment: agencies, for example, widely promote themselves as award winners and showcase their trophies, taking out full-page trade advertising to trumpet their superiority. Reputations are born of the recognition that comes from winning the blue ribbon. Some large agencies consider awards programs to be so important that they maintain special staffs to oversee the submission process and manage the quality and preeminence of their award entries.

In each of these awards programs, the rules for entry explicitly dictate that the program submitted for consideration include a specific, measurable objective based on some form of primary or secondary research. And yet, many judges report that in categories ranging from Special Events to Corporate Communication to Brand Publicity, roughly one out of five entries submitted gets eliminated outright because it contains no underlying research *at all*, and another 50 percent receive substandard marks for stating objectives that would be considered inadequate or incomplete. Given the enormous effort and resources that go into preparing the submissions and the doors to opportunity that open for award-winning agencies, it is remarkable that so many entries are dismissed from consideration as a result of skipping or shortchanging this essential first step.

I now believe that most entrants who omit proper objectives do so not because of oversight but because they are either unable or unwilling to set specific, measurable objectives in the first place. And if so many of the self-proclaimed best programs aren't based on proper objectives, what can be said of the thousands of other PR plans that don't see the light of day or are never submitted for competition and peer review? It seems incredible that companies and brands will invest millions of dollars in PR without a definable understanding of what they're striving to achieve and what will define measurable success. And even if they choose to invest in vague objectives once, why do they continue to make the same risky investments over and over again?

The problem with most stated objectives is that they are so vague they undermine the five reasons listed at the beginning of this chapter. "Deliver media awareness," they say. . . . Or "create significant buzz." Is "generating buzz" rigorous enough to prioritize action? Is there enough of a clear consensus on the definition of *buzz* to avoid dispute? Does *buzz* provide enough structure to act as the foundation for proper PR strategy development and evaluation? At dozens of speeches and conferences around the country, I offer audiences one dollar in exchange for a clear, consensus-formed definition of *buzz*. And that offer is topped by a ten-dollar prize if they can tell me how to measure its results in such a way as to know if "buzz significance" has been achieved. I first made this offer three years ago, and I've yet to pay out a cent. To be fair, the Buzz Marketing Association now has a serious effort under way—but despite their best efforts, the "generate buzz" objective is vague and overused; not the specific, meaningful, and measurable objective that those who invest in PR should insist upon.

That many PR departments and agencies make do without clear and measurable objectives could be the result of a variety of reasons, including lack of budget, lack of understanding as to how objectives are set or why they are important, preference for the creative rather than the quantitative, or apprehension about initiating a score-card process. Whatever the truth may be—and I'm sure that there are many more reasons than these—when it comes to setting objectives by which performance can be precisely evaluated and perpetually refined, many PR people simply choose not to do it.

The Difficulty of Speaking "PR"

One of the challenges facing the public relations profession is the need for a common lexicon like those used in the medical, legal, and accounting professions. Not that dictionaries for public relations don't exist, they do. (In fact, Don Stacks of The University of Miami has brought together an extraordinarily thorough compendium, the *Dictionary of Public Relations Measurement and Research*, which is available through the Institute for Public Relations.) The trouble is the gap between having a dictionary and having a living, common language: the definitions exist, but few abide by them.

One area that may be inhibiting the wider acceptance of serious objectives-setting efforts is the common confusion surrounding the definitions of and the differences between the words *goals* and *objectives*, which are often (and erroneously, in my opinion) used interchangeably. For the purposes of this discussion, it's useful to draw some boundaries.

Goals

Goals are relatively vague, reflecting aspirations rather than a chosen destination. They often appear in the form of organizational vision and mission statements. Unfortunately, although vision and mission statements are important for focusing resources and for ensuring that the PR program's efforts blend with those of the larger organization, they are often indeterminate and difficult to measure. The nature of mission statements thus makes it difficult or even impossible to determine whether or not you've achieved success. For example, goals like "being the best" or "achieving leadership" are unhelpful when it comes time to evaluate PR on either a campaign or program basis.

Objectives

By contrast, *objectives* are measurable and unambiguous so that you—and everyone else—can see when you've met or exceeded them. Business objectives tend to relate to specific standards of business performance and they can be translated quite directly to public relations objectives. PR objectives can and should be specified in terms of *audience* (who is the best target?), *time frame* (when should the program begin and end?), and *outcomes*, which may be further reflected in terms that are *behavioral* (did they do what we wanted them to do?), *attitudinal* (do they feel about us what we wanted them to feel?), and *informational* (do they know about us what we want them to know?). These elements are used to ensure that objectives are specific and success can be quantified when the campaign ends. Research-based objectives are set and evaluated by using the tools discussed in Chapter Three. In so doing, one must ensure that objectives are meaningful, reasonable, and measurable . . . the keys to demonstrating a clear ROI and reducing the risk that your claim to success might be challenged once the program is completed.

Moving from Goals to Objectives

Business goals—even vague, aspirational goals—can be transformed into specific objectives. Take, for example, the following positioning statement from Patagonia, the socially and environmentally conscious (not to mention "successful, category-defining") clothing manufacturer and retailer:

> Committed to Uncommon Culture: We prefer the human scale to the corporate, vagabonding to tourism, the quirky and lively to the toned-down and flattened-out. We used to call our own world of alpinists and surfers a dirtbag culture: of temp jobs and long summers; of foraged meals and tribal travel that followed the seasons, from summer climbs in Yosemite to Baja's winter surfbreaks to spring kayaking. And if many of us now work more than we climb, and care more for our families than for bumming about, we still sound our appeal to the dirtbag within, the need for the wild dirtbag spirit to survive in our e'd-out culture.

I buy Patagonia products and I understand and like what they stand for (could I have a dirtbag within me?), but I'd find the company's "Commitment to Uncommon Culture" statement difficult to translate directly into something specific and measurable even if the words speak directly to customers and employees. But just as any good business goal should do, Patagonia's provides strong guidance for communicators because it can be translated into tightly defined public relations objectives. For example, it offers strong, communicable themes and visual cues, clear ideals that translate to market segments, and obvious prompts for special events and spokespeople. Thus the aspirations represented by Patagonia's cultural statement can be converted into clear and measurable objectives such as "increase awareness of Patagonia as the home of 'dirtbag culture' by 10 percent among 'latent dirtbags' by the end of the year." Presumably, the promotion of "dirtbag culture" translates to sales growth and profitability, if not for the sake of the business then for the sake of the many philanthropic activities that Patagonia supports through its business activities.

Using Research to Set Objectives

Let us begin the discussion of *objectives* by looking at how the research instruments introduced in Chapter Three can be applied in the creation of scientific, meaningful objectives. The purpose of using research and analysis at the beginning of a program is to assess the current public relations environment, to identify opportunities, and to set objectives in light of the environment you find and the opportunities you seek. Your initial research should be based on preliminary program hypotheses whose proof should provide you with the means to answer these key questions: *What is the current environment? What place do we hold within the current environment? Why is this so? Is it likely to continue? What do we need to know now so that we can improve our position?* After the data are compiled, they should be analyzed, interpreted, and shared so that the results can be applied for greater understanding of what's come before and toward improved planning going forward. The metrics associated with the current environment—the quantity and quality of marketing and public relations outputs as well as existing levels of awareness, attitudes, and behavior—are the metrics by which you will set your objectives at the beginning of the programming process, measure program progress during the program, and assess performance at the conclusion.

Using research as part of the objectives-setting process also allows you to pretest some early notions and validate others before allocating resources. What is more, research and analysis reduce the risk of failure since you have a chance to learn from the general and competitive landscape before you begin: you can adapt to and adopt from the best and the worst of what you learn to ensure that your program accomplishes what it is designed to accomplish and avoids the pitfalls of those failed PR programs that came before you.

Using Attitudinal Research to Set Objectives

To set objectives that are meaningful, measurable, and reasonable, surveys are valuable because they reflect the levels of awareness, attitudes, understanding, preference, and behavior that your public relations program seeks to raise. A variety of qualitative and quantitative research tools are useful in setting objectives, including focus groups, consumer surveys, journalist surveys, and executive audits.

Focus Groups. As discussed in Chapter Three, focus groups can help shape quantitative research during the objectives-setting phase. The focus group provides access to the opinions and attitudes of a small group through the give-and-take of an in-depth moderated discussion. Focus groups help you establish "color" and "language" in a relatively short time, thereby providing useful guidelines when creating the quantitative research described next. While the focus group process precedes the objective-setting process, the results directly feed into how you word your objectives as stated in the ensuing consumer survey.

Consumer Surveys. Understanding how to affect your target audience positively is the key to successful public relations. Typically, a survey is conducted at the earliest planning stages of "clean slate" PR program development for the purpose of setting objectives. Your survey ought to explore different areas, through the use of what is known as a "battery of questions." To ensure that you learn what is needed through your survey, include the following batteries:

• *Aided and Unaided Awareness. Unaided* awareness is a measure of recognition without any prompting from the survey (*when you think of a cookie, what kind of cookie comes to mind?*); *aided* awareness is a measure of recognition with the help of survey prompts (*have you ever heard of a Fig Newton?*). The formation and continuance of company and brand awareness is one of the most elementary (and most important) objectives of public relations. Hence, one should gauge levels of awareness *in advance* of the PR program so that awareness levels *after the program* can be compared to that baseline. Public relations is arguably more powerful in building awareness than any other form of marketing communication, and so "building awareness" is commonly found among public relations objectives. A PR campaign can be considered a success when increased awareness is accomplished within a predetermined time frame and budget. In the cases of both *aided* and *unaided* awareness, preexisting levels must be determined so that specific, reasonable, and meaningful awareness targets can be set for assessing your success.

These measures are common whenever "pre- and post-communication" awareness research is undertaken: they provide guidance when tracking changes in awareness and the extent to which they may be attributed to the PR campaign. For example, if you can show that brand awareness is higher among those who are aware of the campaign than among those not aware of the campaign, then it can be reasoned that the PR campaign is contributing to brand awareness. Conversely, if brand awareness is rising while awareness of the PR campaign is declining or is nonexistent, then you could surmise that the public relations initiative is probably not the cause.

• *Respondent Profile.* As part of every questionnaire, ask questions regarding the respondent's personal attributes such as gender, age, geographic location, and income. Some of this information may be requested right at the beginning of the interview process to determine if the respondent is indeed relevant: if, for example, the survey is part of a PR program intent on selling men's shaving cream, the responses of women and fully bearded men may muddle assessment of the objectives of your program. Better to clarify that you're speaking with a man and then ask a quick question such as "Do you shave your beard at least three times each week?" And if the answer is "no," say "thanks," disengage, and reach out to the next potential respondent. If your respondents do fit your target criteria, then you'll know that responses will be helpful in setting objectives and strategy. Usually, a more in-depth battery of questions at the end of the survey supports more detailed "respondent profiling." These factors are extremely valuable when setting target audience objectives and for comparing results after the program. Success will be based on the degree to which the target audience response moves in a favorable direction.

• *Media Consumption Habits.* When gathering information through your survey, it is important to confirm your respondents' media preferences. Ask which media they read, watch, and listen to, and also get an idea of their level of involvement. (Do you watch this show from beginning to end or do you flip channels? Do you read every issue of this newspaper? How often do you visit this site? How long do you wait to read the magazine after receiving it?) Involvement is an important and underutilized criterion for media selection: I religiously read the *New York Times*, but I don't have time to read it front-to-back; I also read my hometown weekly paper and I take in every page . . . sometimes I read it twice during the same week. Finally, it is recommended that you ask where the respondent goes to find new information: the print or online version, the ads, the tear-out inserts, or the editorial content. The answers to these questions will help set the stage for media objectives and for evaluating media results during the postprogram evaluation phase. Depending on whether you have access to the demographics databases described in Chapter Three, you may find that these media questions aren't a good use of the limited amount of time you'll have with the respondent. But if you have this information from one source or another, when it comes time to evaluate your results, you can show the extent to which you hit the media with the highest penetration among the target demographic.

Journalist Surveys. As described in Chapter Three, the Journalist Audit is a way to better understand the needs and preferences of key journalists, and then, once identified, to meet or exceed their expectations. Your survey research will help you create a target media list. Typically, each of your target media will have a journalist assigned to cover your subject area; even small local newspapers and TV news programs have dedicated journalists to cover business, lifestyles, and the arts, and may also have journalists assigned to cover technology, health, and home.

It is important to identify target journalists during this initial research-based objectives phase. If they are worth targeting, their reporting tendencies will be worth tracking in the news content analysis described in the next section. We've seen cases where journalists are predisposed to a particular brand within a category even when all things appear equal. Once you've evaluated the reporting of particular journalists, it is important to compare their coverage of your organization against that of your competitors. If a journalist is running your competitor's news, and it's comparable, you've got a problem that needs fixing. If, on the other hand, the journalist runs neither your material nor your competitor's, it may be something else entirely, such as an improperly targeted journalist.

If the media analysis doesn't reveal any meaningful patterns, consider speaking with the journalist, either during your annual survey or directly if time doesn't permit the luxury of an annual schedule. Sometimes, the media analysis reveals only the symptoms and the journalists provide the cure. More often than not, it is a matter of something simple and fixable: the journalist prefers e-mail when you've been leaving voice mail, or the journalist prefers a local angle that may have to be customized in the future.

Executive Audits. The Executive Audit is of critical importance during the objectives-setting phase since it is imperative that the people who will be either funding or evaluating your program sign off in advance on your objectives. After all, they will later be the ones who determine the extent to which you have met or exceeded your objectives. Their response to questions about business goals and objectives as well as their ideas on how PR can help achieve the organization's overall goals and objectives will be critical in shaping your PR program. You may well find that some executives believe that the objective of the PR program is to generate a high volume of news coverage while others believe the objective should be keeping the company out of the news. These conflicts need to be resolved before objectives can be set.

Using News Content Analysis to Set Objectives

News content analysis is a powerful tool for setting specific and measurable public relations objectives. The content analysis process helps you identify current levels of media exposure as well as uncover key opportunities. At the objectives-setting stage, these are the key determinants for a successful "preprogram" news content analysis:

- Target media frequency
- Key message delivery and quality
- Target audience demographics
- News coverage trends by reporter
- Spokespeople and third-party citations
- Tactics tracking
- Impact Score and Net Effect

Target Media Frequency. During this planning and objectives-setting stage, surveys supplemented by the Media Demographic Audit described in Chapter Three will have identified the audiences you seek as well as the media they favor. Once your target media are identified, a content analysis of news coverage will reveal how often your topic has been covered—as it relates to your company and brand, but also in terms of your competitors. In the case of newspapers, for example, you can track the frequency of coverage by newspaper and by market so that target volume of coverage can be set: "Improve the incidence of positive coverage in the New York market by 20 percent during the next six months" is an example. Typically, target media volume objectives are best set based on your own past performance, your key competitors' performance, and that of "the best in class." The objective is based on measurably improving the frequency with which target media cover your company or brand compared to reporting in the past and reporting of your competitors and peers.

Key Message Delivery and Quality.   In the objectives-setting stage, it is important to assess the many possibilities to determine which messages will be your priority. The content analysis of messages will identify the extent to which various messages are performing in the current and recent media landscape. If one of the messages you are considering for your campaign is already owned by a competitor, you may seek to identify an equally credible and important message that you can own outright. If you find that one theme is being applied negatively to your organization, a priority may be to fix it.

In some cases, company and brand news will also contain or be surrounded by related issues and unintended news coverage that will need to be factored into your objectives. For example, a public relations program promoting a new, cleaner gasoline may have to contend with issues-driven rather than brand-driven news about the high price of fuel or global warming. It is important to uncover these issues and to have contingency plans to deal with them.

Once levels of news coverage are determined, objectives can be set in terms of a specific percentage gain or beating the competition by a specific differential.

Target Audience Demographics.   Another meaningful objective is to reach a greater share of the target audience than your competitors. By conducting the Media Demographic Audit as described in Chapter Three, you will have a way to assess target audience penetration by conducting a content analysis of those media that matter. If the results indicate it would be useful to do so, you can focus your resources on achieving supremacy on just these media, letting your competitors waste their resources on less targeted media outlets.

News Coverage Trends by Reporter. Once the target media are identified, you can track reporter by-lines to focus your resources on the journalists that matter. The content analysis can help you identify which reporters already favor your organization or brand as well as those you may target for improvement. If certain journalists seem to prefer your competitors, determine if your story is as credible and as compelling and reach out to these journalists. The purpose is to improve relationships rather than to blackball your critics, and the ability to earn a place as a journalist's preferred source of information can be a great asset, one that can be definitively measured through content analysis.

Spokespeople and Third-Party Citations. The content analysis can be set up in such a way as to identify the experts journalists cite when writing about your organization and your category. You may also find that these experts favor your company—or your competitors. Once you know who is being cited, you can include these opinion leaders in your objectives, either to refine relations with those opinion leaders who already favor you or to improve relations with those who favor your competitors.

You should also track who at your organization and among your competitors, peers, and opposition are cited as spokespeople. Accessible and responsive spokespeople are a great asset for improving the frequency and quality of news coverage about your organization. Use content analysis at this preprogramming stage to identify who your competitors use as spokespeople and how they perform. There is no better way to engage your organization's own executives than to compare their coverage to what their competitors are generating: executives are typically a competitive group and the more engaged they are, the better your performance will be as your spokespeople help you meet or beat your objectives.

Tactics Tracking. In addition to tracking the best and worst of your own tactical performance, content analysis can identify the tactics of your competitors—both successful and unsuccessful—so that you can create uniquely successful events, sponsorships, and campaigns of your own. Your competitors' least successful tactics probably never see the light of day, but you may find criticism or negative reviews if you look for them. At least you'll be able to avoid the most obvious fiascos while learning about the most successful alternatives. (After reading Chapter Five, remember to ask yourself if you'll be suggesting a giant ice-pop publicity stunt in June.) Once you've identified the best and the worst, set measurable objectives based on what you learn and in such a way as to distinguish your campaign from the rest.

Impact Score and Net Effect. The Impact Score and Net Effect, introduced in Chapter Three, are distilled measures of public relations quality in the media. Analyzing news coverage at this more granular level gives you more specific objectives to set and more ways to achieve success. Look for ways to generate more visuals than your competitors or more exclusive stories and you will see your Impact Score improve. Enlist executives in your organization to be more open and accessible to the media and you'll see the quantity and quality of your media programs improve.

Rules for Setting Good Objectives

Remember our definition of an objective: an objective specifies an *audience* (who is the best target?), a *time frame* (when should the program begin and end?), and one or more *outcomes*, which are *behavioral* (did they do what we wanted them to do?), *attitudinal* (do they feel about us what we wanted them to feel?), or *informational* (do they know about us what we want them to know?). Good objectives aren't hard to set.

Lay the Groundwork

Begin by specifying your desired PR outputs, PR outcomes, and business results—the building blocks for PR success. Let's define each component and then discuss how they can be applied individually and collectively for the purpose of setting objectives:

- *Outputs:* The definition of *output* is not consistent across the PR field. Some define outputs as press releases, special events, collateral materials, and Web sites. Others say these are not outputs but activities; real outputs are found in the media coverage generated as a result of these activities. In this book, I will use this second definition. *Output* objectives look like this:

  "Increase competitive share of positive news coverage by 20 percent by June."

  "Improve our ranking in the 'Delahaye Index' by five places in the annual review."

  "Generate a minimum of 1,000 page visits a month to our Web site's journalist newsroom."

- *Outcomes:* Outcomes are recognized widely in the form of awareness, understanding, attitudes, preference, and behavior. Outcomes are achieved as a result of outputs and, simply put, have an effect on the minds of the target audience. *Outcome* objectives look like this:

  "Boost brand awareness in our top ten markets by 15 points in six months."

  "Increase the perception of our brand as 'the high-quality brand' by 15 percent in the second fiscal quarter versus the first fiscal quarter."

  "Generate ten test-drives during the 'July 4th Sell-a-thon' at each District Seven car dealership."

- *Business results:* Business results are commonly recognized as effects that make a direct contribution toward the organization's goals and objectives. They relate to what happens as a result of outputs and outcomes. *Business results–based* objectives look like this:

  "Use PR to add 1 percent to overall unit sales in the first six months of 2006."

  "Lower PR costs by 15 percent by August."

"[Now that we're in for a potential crisis], use PR to stabilize stock price by working with financial analysts and tracking their comments during the initial phases."

Each example of an output, outcome, or business result is specific and measurable. The degree to which PR activities lead to outputs that lead to outcomes that lead in turn to business results depends on how well you have researched the cause-and-effect relationships among them. Only internal dialogue among business and PR decision makers will confirm if these steps are meaningful in the context of the organization's overall goals and objectives. This is the conversation that should take place once your preplanning surveys and content analysis are done.

Define Useful Objectives

Be sure that your objectives are a guide to action rather than a chronicle of activity: "Send out press releases," "book TV interviews," or "host opinion leaders at a special event" are activities that might help one meet an objective, but they aren't objectives, per se. Activities should be tracked in their own right as measures of productivity. But demonstrating that you have sent out 20 percent more press releases than last year offers not a clue about whether these releases met their objectives. A special event, in isolation, doesn't mean anything unless it satisfies specific criteria. And the TV interview is meaningless if the program is not seen by the people you're targeting or if the interview doesn't allow the interviewee to deliver the key messages of the campaign. So, while these examples qualify as a tactics to-do list, simply having done something shouldn't qualify as having met an objective. In and of themselves, such actions aren't satisfying any of the organization's business goals or objectives.

Remember, objectives emphasize ends rather than means: if any of your objectives begin with words like *distribute* or *create*, then you don't have an objective, you have part of a tactical plan. Good objectives identify outputs, outcomes, and business results rather than tasks, strategies, or deliverables. The latter may be important in helping to achieve the desired results, but they are simply the means by which the end is achieved.

Instead, think of what outcome a particular strategy or supporting tactic is designed to stimulate. Suppose Cameron Cookie Company seeks to increase sales and market share of its Beasty Graham brand by 5 percent in the third fiscal quarter. Sending out press releases might or might not foster objectives like "Generate stories using our three key messages (Beasty Grahams taste great; we use only the best natural ingredients; Cameron's Beasty Graham-brand cookies are essential to a healthy diet) in key media." If the releases are properly targeted, Cameron Beasty Graham stories will appear in media with the highest penetration among health-conscious mothers in markets where Cameron-brand Beasty Grahams are sold, thus satisfying a PR objective such as "Increase news coverage by 80 percent within our top ten markets." And the press releases can be timed for late August and early September so as to be the healthy snack mothers prefer when they pack school lunches for their kids, to satisfy a PR objective such as "raise awareness by 5 percent among parents with kids in elementary school during the back-to-school period."

The sequence suggested is one of audience identification, media targeting, message development, and campaign timing: when properly conceived and productively executed, the PR campaign for Cameron-brand cookies may result in a spike in sales within the markets where stories appear, thus satisfying Cameron's business objective for increased sales and market share during the third fiscal quarter.

In the case of "sponsoring a special event for opinion leaders," the event might advance an objective such as "Raise awareness by 10 percent within three months among local elected officials and clergy of our company's business objective to be the community's best corporate citizen through our commitment to local philanthropy." The action suggested in this example is one of audience and influencer identification. And if these PR objectives are met, then the overall objectives of the organization are more likely to be successful.

Set a Specific Time Frame

Sometimes, within certain projects, time frames are predefined. *The Summer Salad Dressings Season Kick-off*, for example, is obviously seasonal in nature. Most PR programs at the corporate and brand levels are ongoing, and use seasonal campaigns as the means to an end. Solid objectives will include a schedule on which general objectives will be met, and the timetable for PR objectives should coincide with the overall business goals of the organization, as we've said before. A toy company that generates 70 percent of its annual sales during the Christmas shopping season, for example, has to plan around that time of year.

The PR schedule should be tied to the organization's general business calendar, with milestones such as traditional sales seasons and fiscal quarters. PR timetables are also tied to professional calendars like the annual meeting or the Acapulco marketing planning retreat in September. Interim targets may be driven by new product introductions and may be scheduled in concert with others involved with managing the organization's brand marketing mix. Such internal events may be the monthly CEO roundtable, when heads of each of the organization's units deliver short-term results to senior management. To be able to report results at proper intervals, one must have objectives that clearly translate to these time frames. Be sure to speak with others in the organization to ensure that PR's objectives support theirs, and vice versa. As in the case of every objective, it is important to get agreement from those who fund PR programs that they see the calendar you've identified as meaningful, sufficiently measurable, and reasonable.

Differentiate long-term objectives from short-term objectives. While it is important for business and PR departments alike to have objectives, some objectives are difficult to achieve wholesale and can only be accomplished in an incremental fashion. A small start-up that has a long-term goal of capturing at least half of its target market will usually set incremental objectives, such as increasing market share every year for the next five years. Similarly, long-term PR objectives need to be translated into shorter-term objectives, usually on an annual basis.

Construct your objectives with respect to and in recognition of what PR can and cannot accomplish reasonably, whether in the near term or the long term. Public relations can be a powerful agent but it can't accomplish the impossible. Setting objectives that are unreasonable is a waste of time and resources for everyone and, worse, may prevent more appropriate alternative endeavors from taking hold. One way to determine what is reasonable is to benchmark against competitors and your own past performance. During your clean-slate PR start-up this may be difficult, but it can be done. Once benchmark performance levels have been established, PR objectives should become more and more reasonable—and more accurate—over time.

Identify Specific Media

For the most part, PR audience identification is a highly subjective exercise rather than the scientific process that it is—*and should be*—in other areas of marketing communication. Audience targeting is inherent in direct marketing, which is predicated on its ability to deliver pinpoint communication to the proper recipient, and it is also a primary consideration in advertising. However, audience identification has not traditionally been central to public relations objectives, even though targeting is just as fundamental to successful PR as it is to other forms of successful marketing. This may be explained by the different natures of paid versus nonpaid communication: the risk with nontargeted paid advertising is that millions of dollars are on the line; in the case of PR, which can distribute press releases through inexpensive commercial newswires, the risk for broad and vague target media objectives is considerably less. However, it should be said that an unfocused outlay of human, financial, and creative resources will certainly undermine the likelihood of PR success, just as it would in any other endeavor.

Proper audience and media identification for the purposes of setting objectives also takes into account the size of the audience. The audience size doesn't in itself determine the importance of the program. An extreme example would be a PR plan designed to help sell hydroelectric turbines, where the PR department might have ten trade media targets and might hope to sell a dozen turbines each year. Within this context, it would be unreasonable to construct media relations objectives around generating hundreds of positive turbine-focused trade media stories a month; fifty stories a year might be a stretch in such a narrowly focused industry as hydroelectric power generation. And since the buying decision is so involved, it would be an even bigger stretch to attempt making the link between media relations–driven PR and sales. However, a public relations plan designed to sell bottled water may have an audience of many millions with media targets among hundreds (even thousands) of consumer media. In a mature competitive market like bottled water, a campaign promoting a new brand might have to generate thousands of high-quality stories in targeted media to have an impact on consumers and to make a meaningful contribution to the brand's sales objective. The fifty-story-a-year goal of the turbine manufacturer would not make a dent on mass-market awareness for advancing the sales of bottled water.

Define Your Audience Relationship

You need to know what your relationship is with the audience and how you want that relationship to change. Do you want your PR campaign to build loyalty among existing customers or steal customers from your competitors? For example, cola drinkers in Memphis are extraordinarily loyal to Coca-Cola. A new soft drink targeting Memphis would have its work cut out if the new brand was not sufficiently and compellingly distinctive from the overwhelming market leader. A battle for Memphis market share might require more funding or more time than would be needed in a target market that reveals no such loyalty. It is also worth exploring what sort of relationship the company or brand wants to have with its target audience. Is the objective defined by sales or legislative support? Preprogramming research should be used to uncover the existing relationship with the company and its competitors. Many smart PR planners borrow from market research conducted by other units within the company to uncover these relationships, but it can be an expensive proposition.

Less expensive than custom market research are demographics databases like the Media Audit, which aren't regularly applied to public relations objectives, strategy development, or evaluation. Databases with which we're familiar offer hundreds of criteria by which audience relationships can be determined. It may be easy, for example, to identify Memphis as a "cola market," but you need to know whether Memphis cola drinkers are your customers, prospective customers, or a competitor's loyalists.

Ensuring Top Management Buy-In to PR Objectives

Following the rules outlined thus far will ensure that your objectives are measurable and meaningful, but it won't guarantee that they will ensure top management support or align with the organization's goals (although it ought to be very close unless other areas of the business aren't as thorough as you've been). Savvy PR professionals make sure that their PR objectives further larger organizational goals and objectives and take other positive steps to secure top management backing.

Tie Your Objectives to the Organization's Goals and Objectives

Beyond assessing your customers' preferences (I'll tell you now: they all want three scoops of ice cream for a nickel), it is essential to know the mission of your organization before defining your own objectives, and similarly, the organization's goals and objectives should be reflected in good PR objectives. Because public relations objectives must be aligned with the organization's goals and objectives, it is critically important that the PR planner understand fully the organization's priorities in terms of strengths, weaknesses, opportunities, and threats, also known by the acronym *SWOT analysis*. PR's SWOT analysis of the organization should extend well beyond the traditional PR purview to include factors such as financial performance, corporate and brand reputation, vision and leadership, workplace environment, and corporate citizenship.

A publicly held consumer-products company, for example, would probably have goals in multiple areas. No doubt it has sales, revenue, and profit targets. But it might also be eager to attract and keep its most talented employees, to boost its reputation on Wall Street as a worthwhile investment, and to keep competitors on the defensive. Business goals such as these can be readily translated into business objectives (increase sales volume by 20 percent; attract at least two of the Medill School's top marketing graduates; raise the stock price to $35 per share and keep it there through the rest of the year; gain market share against the competition, and so on).

Business objectives such as these can also be translated into measurable PR objectives. For example, each of these themes is directed to a particular audience, whether it is the consumer marketplace, employees and prospective employees, or Wall Street analysts, investors, and financial reporters. What is more, each of these audiences can be the focus of communication outreach seeking to stimulate a point of view that the company and its audiences alike would consider to be mutually favorable.

The process by which one sets PR objectives that tie in with the organization's overall business goals begins with knowing and understanding them before setting PR objectives. Before confirming the perceptions and preferences of your executives via the first

Executive Audit, you can find this information on the organization's Web site, in its annual report, its employee newsletter, and the like. Using what was defined earlier as "secondary research," you could begin simply by identifying and listing your organization's goals and objectives, and then accompanying each of the overall goals and objectives with a corollary PR objective.

Once the business's goals and objectives are viewed as the environment that helps to shape PR objectives, the next step is to gain an understanding of how other communications disciplines within the organization are interpreting business objectives toward their own advertising, promotions, or other marketing and communication objectives. Reach out to leaders in these areas to learn more about how they interpret the way the organization's business goals apply to their own endeavors.

Make Sure You Have Buy-In from Senior Management

In Chapter Three, we introduced the Executive Audit, a qualitative research instrument by which perceptions, attitudes, and preferences toward PR can be uncovered. The Executive Audit, which ensures confidentiality to the participants and thereby a high degree of candor, helps PR people understand how the PR function is viewed within the organization, but it also helps to set objectives in the ways described in this chapter. A structured approach based on the Executive Audit assures that you find out everything you need to know. Show key executives all three sets of goals and objectives: business goals, business objectives, and the corresponding PR objectives, and then discuss them, refine them, and get agreement. Confirm your understanding of the business goals and objectives of the organization as well as of the target audiences, the time frame, and the actions and activities, long-term objectives, and subordinate short-term objectives . . . in other words, double-check on each of the objectives discussed in this chapter.

But before cutting your PR objectives in stone, it is important to confirm one additional level of understanding, and that is how executives currently view the PR operation and how they will evaluate your success. The Executive Audit is structured to deliver on three dimensions: what is important for PR to deliver, the extent to which the PR department delivers on these standards now, and finally, the extent to which the PR department delivers compared to competitors. The answers to these questions will round out the objective-setting process, and they will guide PR planning so that the results address the measures agreed to at this preliminary stage.

Conclusion

Unfortunately, some PR people prefer to handicap their company's or their client's PR program rather than take the risk of putting hard, measurable objectives in place so that they can be scientifically evaluated later. They'd rather have their managers or their clients not know for sure if the program succeeded or failed than risk jeopardizing their standing. I would argue that refusal to set specific goals is a form of malpractice, especially when you consider the affordable new tools at hand, the newfound recognition and still huge upside for PR, and the increasing scope of activities for which PR people are now held responsible. But then again, responsibility is also borne by those who fund PR programs. Until those executives who invest in PR programs demand solid, specific, measurable objectives, change is unlikely to come. And as long as so many practitioners within the public relations profession avoid the establishment of serious, scientific objectives, they will continue to find themselves searching for their seat at the decision-making table in a state of uncertainty and anxiety.

If you are investing in public relations, you have a right to ask some hard questions. What is more, you have the right to expect a detailed explanation of how the answers to each question were determined.

Questions Every PR Investment Decision Maker Should Ask

- Are our PR objectives related to our business goals and objectives? How was this determined?
- Have we set our objectives using a clean-slate approach? How?
- Are our objectives meaningful, reasonable, and measurable? How so?
- Have we segmented long-term and short-term objectives? How so?
- Do our objectives specify outputs, outcomes, and business results?
- Have we identified the optimal audience?
- Has everyone with a stake in the game signed off on the objectives?

5

Using Research to Shape Public Relations Strategy and Tactics

Objectives are the strong foundation upon which public relations programs are designed, executed, and evaluated, but you still need to develop and execute a strategy for achieving them. Strategy, in turn, requires the proper deployment of tactics. In the real world of public relations, strategic success is accomplished through a special combination of expert talent, long-term vision, and analytic proficiency, and tactical success is achieved through superior creativity, dogged execution, and a keen understanding of the overriding strategy. With effective research, you can achieve strategic and tactical success—delivering on your organization's strengths, speaking to your target audience's interests and concerns, and clearly differentiating yourself from the competition.

Putting aside Edward Bernays's original and ambitious definition of public relations as a social science, most of what constitutes "practical everyday PR" focuses on generating visibility through tactical rather than strategic planning. To this day, "managing the media" consumes the resources of most PR departments and agencies, whether they aim to gain visibility in the media or to reduce it. But to what end? In recent times, the public relations profession has asserted its place at the table by offering more than just mere publicity. At the same time, occupants of the C-suite have grown to embrace the importance of managing reputation and of effective communication. As a result, there has grown a mutual expectation from within PR and from among those who invest in PR to develop greater capabilities to drive the organization forward rather than simply generating visibility for its own sake.

Despite the fact that most everyday PR activity focuses on tactics, the tendency within most PR circles is to overemphasize the strategic aspects of public relations and to subordinate the tactical. The trend is everywhere. In fact, very few PR agencies of note take pride in their special ability to "generate publicity"—and they are often viewed as second-rate press agents intent on undermining PR's newfound respect. To be taken seriously, it seems, everyone with a PR responsibility feels the need to self-identify as a strategist. This is evident through a bit of unscientific research: A Google search on the phrase "strategic public relations" yields pages and pages of references; among the top thirty items, fifteen PR firms come up with the word *strategic* in their name. "Strategic" has become as generic and ineffectual as the brands found in Roadrunner cartoons: these agencies might as well call themselves "Acme" and "Apex."

A similar Google search on the phrase "tactical public relations" yields a much weaker return with not a single PR firm with "tactical" in its name (although it does yield a link to PRSA's *Tactics*, one of the profession's great trade publications). The implications for PR's heavy emphasis on strategy are clear: strategy is the superior mental and managerial activity and tactics can be relegated harmlessly to the lower echelons. In reality, this argument is simply wrong. Those who take this course will almost certainly end in failure. In the first place, tactics must be fully considered as part of the strategic process if anything is to come as a result of conducting the campaign. In the second place, providing exposure to and involvement in the strategy-development process among lower-ranking staff members brings with it a higher likelihood that the strategy will be evident in every aspect of the campaign.

Strategy and tactics are inextricably intertwined; both are necessary for organizational goals and objectives as well as PR objectives to be achieved. As the Chinese general and philosopher Sun Tzu wrote in 500 B.C., "Strategy without tactics is the slowest route to victory. Tactics without strategy is the noise before defeat." And here lies the paradox: if everyone in PR is a strategist, how does anything get done? And if everyday PR is so tactically focused on simply generating visibility in whatever form, how does anyone achieve meaningful business and PR objectives? Proper balancing is necessary, and research-based public relations can provide the necessary guidance and the underlying structure.

The Difference Between Strategy and Tactics

Just as confusion abounds regarding PR's definition of "setting objectives" and how that differs from "setting goals," as discussed in Chapter Four, the terms *strategy* and *tactics* are often used without proper distinction even by people who believe they know the difference between them. Direct dictionary comparisons are hard to find—within and outside the PR lexicon—but it is generally agreed that strategy and tactics are absolutely connected.

Strategy

Strategy is most often defined in terms related to chess and the military. Simply put, strategy is generalship. The creation of a military campaign is similar to the creation of a public relations campaign: strategists must take into account a variety of factors, including their own current situation and the position of their opponent, their place within a particular environment, and their strengths and weaknesses, as well as calculated alternatives, risks, and timetable. In public relations, PR strategy is a course of action taken to accomplish long-term organizational goals and objectives through the thoughtful and economical deployment of PR tactics. So, for example, a PR strategy might be to launch a new product successfully through public relations tactics that deliver salient messages to the target audience within a given time frame.

The strategy development process fits within the larger constitution of the public relations process. Here are the key steps:

1. *Determine the precise result you want to accomplish.* If you've done a thorough job during the objectives-setting phase, this should be clear to you.

2. *Conduct research to establish a practical starting point that accounts for the environment in which you're operating.* Where is your strategy being applied and how will that place change after your strategy has been executed?

3. *Construct a strategic plan that focuses on the big picture, incorporating objectives and outcomes.* The plan must relate to your organization's business goals and objectives as well as your own long-term PR objectives.

4. *Gain a common understanding among internal clients to build consensus in support of the strategy.* Buy-in is critical at every stage of the public relations process.

5. *Make certain the tactics designed to support the strategy can achieve the business results you're after.* At every stage, your purpose should focus on achieving meaningful business results.

Tactics

Tactics are interim and incremental activities that are aligned with the larger strategy. As such, each tactic is a means to an end rather than the end itself. Using the game of chess as an example, tactics are the board movements and pawn advances by which a player pursues the goals of gaining victory and avoiding defeat. A chess match is played so that the game can be won; the tactic of capturing your opponent's knight may make sense in the short term but not in terms of the overall strategy if the knight is your king's only protection. In public relations, tactics come in the form of press releases, brochures, press conferences, special events, and sponsorships. These tactics are used as vehicles to deliver salient messages to target audiences, and the strategic deployment of tactics gives the program's objectives a much higher likelihood for success.

These tips will help guide you through an effective tactical development process:

1. *Never lose sight of the campaign's strategic goals and objectives, and make sure you understand them.* Tactics must support the communication strategy, *and* they must support the goals and objectives of the organization. Period.

2. *Internalize the objectives and then specify supporting actions designed to deliver on your strategy.* The strategy must be interwoven throughout the tactic. Every press release, interview, and special event should be considered for its ability to drive the achievement of your objectives.

3. *Craft the campaign around specific activities segmented into explicit time frames with explicit outcomes.* If your objectives are segmented by time frame, your tactics should also be segmented by time frame. What is more, the likelihood of your success is greater when the tactic is relevant to the time during which it occurs.

4. *Work to ensure that the tactical activities are well executed.* No explanation needed.

5. *Evaluate performance and relate individual tactics back to the original strategy and the objectives they were designed to achieve.* Every aspect of the program—from beginning to end—must be measurable. It's also worth noting that it can be helpful to demonstrate the achievement of your objectives at every stage of the tactical plan.

Real-World Strategy and Tactics

Here are some examples to help you differentiate a strategy from a tactic for your own purposes. One easy way to distinguish a strategy from a tactic is to consider whether your target market is a given or not: if you are searching the environment, seeking new target markets or looking for subtle changes to your current target markets, then you are preparing a strategic plan. On the other hand, if you start out knowing exactly who your target market is, and your focus is on developing an assortment of activities to reach it, then you are developing a tactical plan.

So here are some descriptions of what strategies and tactics look like, from our own experience and also based on winning entries from PR's most prestigious awards programs.

A PR strategy is based on a theory about how and why things work, whereas a PR tactic is focused on the communication vehicles. The IABC is one of the world's preeminent communications associations. Each year, the IABC's Gold Quill Award recognizes exceptional public relations and communication campaigns. One of this year's "best of the best" was conducted by PR agency Publicis Dialog on behalf of the Hazelnut Council. The objective of the program was to increase consumption of hazelnuts in the United States, using a strategy built on the communication of compelling messages to a target audience of food company decision makers, trade and consumer media, and others. The Hazelnut Council and Publicis Dialog didn't just start targeting consumers with a message; they had a strategy for increasing consumption by targeting food makers to add the nuts to more products. The strategy was to go after consumers indirectly. This example demonstrates how a strategy is always based on a theory about why and how things work, which in business usually means why and how people buy products.

Publicis Dialog began the strategy-development process by conducting both quantitative and qualitative primary research augmented by secondary research to determine the current positioning of the product and the optimal target audience, which they determined to consist of food industry decision makers from candy, bakery, snack food, and ice cream companies. The research stage provided a strong underpinning for the strategy going forward.

Based on the objectives and the strategy, the agency derived specific tactics to serve as vehicles to deliver the campaign's key messages to target audiences: developing and distributing hazelnut marketing kits, improving Web site communications, setting up meetings with food company executives, generating leads through trade shows, creating interest through free hazelnut samples, creating awareness through trade advertising and editorial placements, targeting prominent chefs, encouraging product development through a contest, and so on. Each of these tactics was designed for "communications delivery" in support of hazelnuts. How did the program turn out? The total number of new hazelnut products on store shelves increased 17 percent between 2003 and 2004, according to an independent company called Product Scan Online that tracks cash register data. In addition, five new companies have hazelnut products in development and four companies have actually introduced new hazelnut products—all as a direct result of the campaign.

A strategy seems like a comparatively routine approach to supporting objectives whereas a tactic is often exceptional. A strategy is the process by which one might support the business's objective of improving the company's revenues by X percent and profitability by Y percent. That's a meaningful outcome for a strategy to achieve but it isn't extraordinary in concept. Tactics, if done well, will support such a routine strategy in ways that are much more likely to be exciting and unique. The PR objective is to contribute a fair share to sales. The strategy will dictate message and media planning . . . all pretty standard in marketing PR. The tactic, on the other hand, may require something extraordinary to break through the clutter and achieve widespread, strategy-supporting visibility.

Here's an example of how one company sought to boost sales for a brand of frozen fruit bar. The strategy in and of itself wasn't all that spectacular—a combination of audience and media targeting, message selection, and other familiar elements. The tactic upon which the company decided was a fun and compelling event at which it would create and unveil history's largest ice pop (17.5 tons) to break the Guinness world record. This tactic was employed by Snapple to introduce its new line of ice pops in New York City. Unfortunately (or *fortunately*, as some cynical but publicity-savvy PR people argue), the event was scheduled on a particularly hot summer day, thus creating the world's record for largest ice pop to completely melt in a public park. New York's Union Square was covered in syrupy red goop until it was cleaned up. The story tipped the scales from the news of the world to the news of the weird, but the media reaction to this story was extraordinary—maybe even unique. Snapple worked with the city to return the park to its original state, and among Union Square–loving New Yorkers, it may have been more of a hassle than it was a media event. But it's safe to say that as a result of this campaign, many more people know that Snapple makes frozen fruit bars.

A strategy contains many facets, whereas a tactic is singular. A car company, for example, uses a variety of campaigns to achieve its overall PR objective of boosting sales: events, promotions, sponsorships, and car shows occur throughout the year, each heavily PR-driven. These campaigns may happen at different times and they may employ different platforms. And while they are targeted toward current and prospective car owners, each campaign may segment the target audience among young buyers, sports car lovers, or the environmentally conscious. As a result, messaging and media planning are built on the messages and media that resonate most with each segment within the larger target market. When done properly, the strategy promotes compelling and credible solutions in such a way as to leave competitors in the dust. Objectives are met through a marriage of the strategic and the tactical.

Drawing from the *PR Week* Awards, the winner of the Best Promotional Event of the Year was a General Motors campaign executed in conjunction with PR agency Weber Shandwick. GM approached the months of January and February—typically a slow traffic period for dealerships—with the objective of increasing awareness and pushing more consumers to test its line of automobiles. The strategy was intended to get consumers interested in— and interacting with—both GM cars and the OnStar system. The company hoped that sales would increase and an audience beyond GM's core enthusiasts would get a better perception of the brand. The carmaker created a campaign where one thousand individuals had a chance to win one of GM's fifty-four models by visiting a dealership and pushing the OnStar button.

The campaign involved many facets of tactical PR and marketing in pursuit of the objective, but the PR push centered on the North American International Auto Show, where former NFL star Boomer Esiason kicked off the Sunday CBS pregame show for Wild Card weekend with an on-camera demonstration of the contest. Other tactics included press releases targeting print, television and radio, and Internet news outlets.

By the time the campaign wrapped up, GM determined that it had driven 400,000 incremental customers to its dealers, where more than 2 million people pushed the OnStar button. Additionally, 50 percent of participants said the campaign increased the likelihood that they would purchase a GM vehicle, and 56 percent said it improved their participation with the car manufacturer.

GM sells cars every day of the year, but this strategy to drive showroom traffic, using the contest as a tactic, delivered through a combination of activities including this singular event. It used PR to fulfill meaningful business objectives, and it delivered through the proper execution of multifaceted PR tactics.

A strategy is created to build and sustain a stable advantage, whereas a tactic is designed to accelerate competitive advantage through shorter-term bursts. Because a strategy focuses on the big picture, it is less concerned with the tactical activity burst associated with a particular promotion. However, activity bursts should result in outcome bursts that help to drive the strategy forward. Once these outcome bursts are delivered, it is the strategist's role to sustain them and to build incremental progress upon them. For example, Toyota is widely known as an auto manufacturer of the highest quality: year after year, Toyota models are recognized by critics and in the marketplace as being among the very best. One of Toyota's PR campaigns won the 2004 *PR Week* Award for Best New Product Introduction. If the strategy in this case was to sell more Toyota cars and to reinforce Toyota's image as a manufacturer of high-quality, environmentally friendly automobiles (not a huge assumption), then the tactics provided an extra boost to an already strong brand. In this case, the strategy acknowledged that the Toyota Prius hybrid has long been a market leader and the darling of the entertainment cognoscenti in Hollywood due to its environment-friendly engineering. To build on a celebrated history and to make the message resonate for those beyond the upper echelon, the tactical campaign involved getting influencers and the media behind the wheel to promote the benefits of this nontraditional vehicle.

Toyota, along with PR agency Golin-Harris, chose to unveil the 2004 Prius at the New York Auto Show in April 2003. One interesting tactical aspect of the campaign was participation in the Environmental Media Awards, which gave the company more opportunities to interact with socially conscious celebrities and provided private test drives, which led to twenty-four orders from thirty participants.

The launch generated a significant volume of high-quality news coverage, but more important were the business results: The car went on sale on October 17, 2003, and through a combination of product superiority and marketing, broke monthly sales figures with 4,085 sold. November sales topped 5,500, shattering the record set the month before and representing a 196 percent gain over 2002. Sales targets for 2004 were moved from 36,000 cars to 47,000. As of October 2004, year-to-date orders were up 225 percent from 2003. These are the most recent numbers available, but it seems likely that sales are still going strong.

In this example, the introduction was a tactical activity burst that drove the strategy of using public relations to deliver on the objective of sustained growth.

How to Properly Develop a Scientific Public Relations Strategy

In my opinion, a good public relations strategy begins with the clean-slate objectives process discussed in Chapter Four. Once objectives have been prioritized, the next task is to put the "winning" objectives through three critical applications: audience segmentation, media prioritization, and message engineering. The segmentation, prioritization, and engineering process is a type of strategic public relations SWOT analysis through which the plan can be realized.

Prioritizing Audiences

The first step after setting objectives is to take what you've learned from the preprogram research and objectives-setting process and apply it to the task of prioritizing your audience. Audience targeting is the first and most critical factor in developing a public relations strategy, and as noted, intuition and experience aren't enough to make serious strategic decisions. In-depth, broad-based demographics databases are available for serious audience targeting research, allowing marketers to target by hundreds and even thousands of criteria and combinations. The results are often counterintuitive, as in the case where the optimal target audience for an upscale luxury car wasn't gearheads, motorheads, or racing enthusiasts, it was suburban women of a certain means. Since so much rests on the proper targeting decision, one would think that serious resources go into the task, but typically they do not. Rather than simple rankings based on market population, which are common but can be misleading, we prefer something we call "target market rankings" based on the number of people who fit the target audience profile within the market rather than just the number of people in the market.

To see the importance of target market ranking, consider the ten most populous markets:

Top U.S. Population Centers in 2002

Rank	*Market Name*
1	New York
2	Los Angeles
3	Chicago
4	Philadelphia
5	Boston
6	San Francisco and Oakland

7	Dallas and Fort Worth
8	Washington, D.C.
9	Atlanta
10	Houston

Now consider a target market analysis performed on behalf of a major computer chip manufacturer that wanted to reach a target consisting of people who were aged twenty-five to forty-four years, and who had household income of at least $35,000 annually, one or more children, and a PC.

Top U.S. Target Population Centers for Chip Maker

Rank	Market Name	Targeted Population
1	New York	1,129,000
2	Los Angeles	755,000
3	Chicago	704,000
4	San Francisco	553,000
5	Washington, D.C.	446,000
6	Philadelphia	369,000
7	Dallas	363,000
8	Houston	348,000
9	Detroit	336,000
10	Boston	326,000

The chip maker's list shows how misleading traditional audience targeting methods based on population can be. If the chip maker's PR department focused solely on the top ten markets by general population, as so many do, Detroit would not be targeted even though it is in the real top ten market—the one based on the target audience population. Conversely, too many resources might be devoted to Atlanta simply because it is a top ten population center (even though it is not among the top ten population centers for the target audience). Moreover, the advantage to target audience market selection on a geographic level is by far surpassed when the target audience's *media* selection priorities are revealed.

Whether your focus is on geographic markets or specific media targets, audience prioritization should be built around certain scientific factors. If, for example, you are conducting a consumer PR campaign in support of a marketing effort, consider at least these criteria:

- *Sales potential:* Do people in this group already buy your product or another within the category?
- *Growth potential:* Is this audience segment growing or shrinking?
- *Ability to make purchase decisions:* Can they buy what you're selling?
- *Media exposure:* Do they read, watch, or listen to the media? Which ones?

Once you've determined which audience is most valuable, you are ready to create a media plan that will enable the most efficient and effective communication with the audience you're seeking to reach.

Media Targeting

Media targeting requires serious thinking rather than a big Rolodex file. Ten minutes of audience ideation vetted by "coffee-table logic" won't cut it and neither will broad-based categories such as "women aged fourteen to forty-nine," which is just too big a segment to be meaningful. And in some cases, target audience population centers can be misleading. When you come down to just those media targets that have the highest concentration of exposure among the target audience you've identified, real surprises abound. Continuing with the example of the computer chip manufacturer, the print media with the highest penetration among the target market were (in order) the *Sacramento Bee*, the *Portland Oregonian*, the *Seattle Times*, the *Indianapolis Star*, and the *San Jose Mercury News*—not the *New York Times* (it didn't crack the top fifty; the *Village Voice* had a higher ranking) and not the *L.A. Times* (the *Orange County Register* ranked higher). Some of the more interesting media choices came from among those media with relatively low circulations but with almost 100 percent target audience penetration: the *Deseret News* of Salt Lake City and the *Idaho Statesman* of Boise, Idaho, two cities rarely if ever found on any PR firm's advanced "must have" media target list. Ironically, having a broader base of target media—especially below-the-radar media such as these two examples—provides PR people with many more ways to win. After all, who else is targeting these outlets?

Typically, the trade or business-to-business media offer fewer surprises, if only because there tend to be fewer media possibilities in those fields than in consumer media, and they tend to have a much narrower editorial focus. However, you may see some overlap where, for example, toothpaste manufacturers read the chain-store retailers' newsletter and the toothpaste buyer from Wal-Mart reads the toothpaste trade media. This information can be uncovered during the preprogram consumer and customer research during the "media preferences" battery of questions, and then prioritized during the media targeting phase.

Remember, the only media that matter are those that help you accomplish your objectives. When it comes time to prioritize your media targets in terms of how you allocate precious resources, create a "scientific media strategy plan" along the lines shown in Figure 5.1. The process shown is one by which the Media Demographic Audit results are married to the results of your competitive news content analysis (described in Chapter Three). The demographic audit tells you which media are important but it doesn't tell you which media are more and less receptive to your news. The media analysis alone can tell you which media are more and less receptive

Figure 5.1. Scientific Media Strategy Plan.

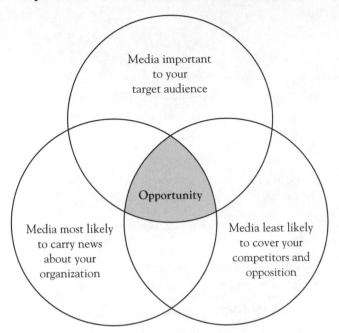

but it doesn't tell you which media have the highest penetration. By combining the two, you can turn data into action.

Message Engineering

A common belief is that PR message creation is a purely creative endeavor. By this point in the book, you know my response: I believe that public relations is as much science as it is art and I further believe that the science upon which effective public relations can be based actually enhances the creative process, by focusing creative resources on the most compelling and credible messages as proven through research.

Message engineering is a scientific, target audience–based process of developing brand, issue, or corporate positioning. In consumer service and product marketing, *positioning* means giving the service or product a meaning in the minds of prospective customers that distinguishes it from other services and products and induces people to want to buy it. The same holds true for positioning corporate image, public affairs, and investor relations, as well as marketing, advertising, promotion, and sales. Here are four "musts" to follow in developing the optimal messaging strategy:

- *You must develop messages with a target audience in mind:* Messaging done without others in mind is a poor use of resources. Always focus on the target and you will know not only what to say but how to say it.

- *You must understand what motivates the target to act:* In this case, *action* can mean to buy, to apply for a job, to invest, to vote your way, and any number of other actions. It is this element that allows you to create messages that are compelling.

- *You must know the degree to which your proposition matches the target audience's priorities and reality:* This refers to your ability to deliver messages that are credible. The focus is simultaneously inward and outward—does your message resonate with the audience, and does your message seem believable coming from you.

- *You must understand how your competition or opposition performs against those needs:* Differentiation is an elementary ingredient in the communication mix.

These four elements help ensure that your message strategy will account for what's important to your target audience and how you deliver on what's important, versus how your competitors deliver on what's important. A thorough analysis of these elements will reveal your chance for breakthrough messaging. The overlapping circles shown in Figure 5.2 illustrate this process perfectly: at the point of overlap, you find opportunity.

Message engineering is an example of how science and creativity come together to make for more effective public relations. The

Figure 5.2. Scientific Message Strategy Plan.

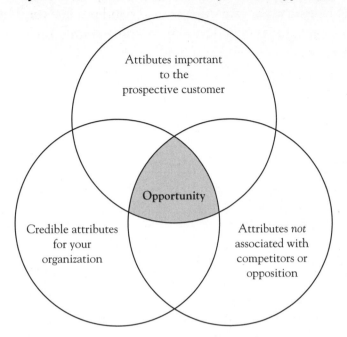

message engineering process has four stages, the first of which drives the rest.

The initial step in message engineering uses qualitative research in the form of a focus group to generate a multitude of propositional attributes and benefits—messaging opportunities—including future options as well as current approaches. For a retail clothing chain, such attributes and benefits might look like this: we have the latest fashions, we have the widest selection, our salespeople are friendly, and so on. Once the list is developed, the group decides on which of many possibilities are the most likely to succeed, selecting twenty-five or so to test through quantitative research.

The second step is the survey stage, in which the twenty-five attributes and benefits are scientifically tested using a telephone survey to interview no fewer than three hundred respondents (the higher the number, up to about a thousand, the more reliable the outcome). The survey questionnaire should include the following components:

- Product category attitudes and experience, including involvement in the purchase process, attitudes and practices with regard to purchase, and purchase patterns and brand preferences.

- Purchase and selection criteria rating of the twenty-five winning attributes and benefits in terms of desirability.

- Awareness and usage, brands recognized, brands purchased, share of purchase in past year, most frequently purchased.

- Perceptions of competing brands, including ratings of competitors and your brand in terms of the same twenty-five attributes and benefits along with potential openness to other brands.

- New messaging concept evaluation, describing fully the new concept and then asking for opinions.

- Media habits—since much of public relations is driven by editorial treatment, determine the best media vehicles for your new positioning in terms of media credibility, involvement, and impact.

- Demographics—to determine the optimal target audience, ask questions that will allow you to create a demographic profile based on what you learn.

Once the interviewing is complete, the third step of the process begins: a formal analysis designed to explore the three or four major drivers revealed during the second step, to uncover the derivation and intensity of the prospect's needs, and to get a clear picture of the competitive environment. If this process were to be mapped, it would look like the diagram shown in Figure 5.3.

This example shows the message engineering process as it might be applied to a large retail chain. In a real study, the bottom row of boxes would show all twenty-five attributes and benefits tested, but the figure simplifies it by showing only the first two in detail. Of these, "widest selection" is clearly a key driver: prospects consider

Figure 5.3. Message Engineering.

Large Retail Chain

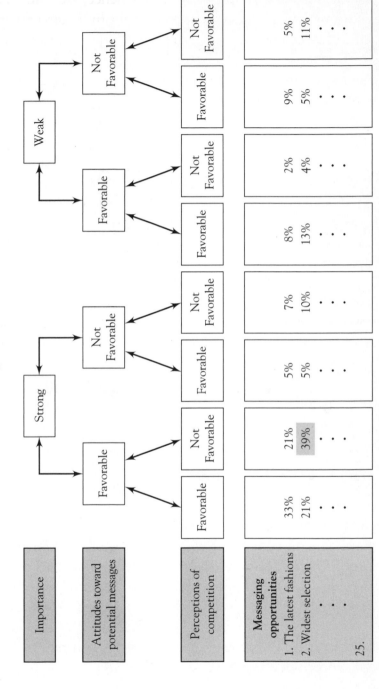

this attribute important, see it as credible when delivered by your company, and do not see your competitors as credible when delivering this message.

Several distinctive target audiences should result, each of which has its own three or four winning messages. A message may be just one or several words; in fact, a message strategy may be just a few sentences about your organization or brand that you want to have imprinted in the minds of your target audiences. Target these audiences through the media they find most credible and most involving and deliver a message that is clear, concise, and impressive.

The fourth and final step in the message strategy development stage is to conduct a content analysis of news coverage originating in those media with the highest penetration among the target audience. The purpose is to determine the extent to which the three or four winning messages are delivered by your company and your competitors, as shown in Figure 5.2. Smart PR planners give the highest priority to those messages that are important to the target audience, viewed as favorable aspects of the sponsoring company, and are not associated favorably with competitors.

Once the landscape is known, invest your tactical resources on those activities that deliver the winning messages and in the media that matter to the audience you're trying to reach.

Why the Strategy Development Process Goes Wrong

When public relations programs fail to perform at the intended level of achievement, a number of things should be considered. Ideally, public relations investment decision makers should consider these sources of potential downfall before authorizing any PR spending:

- The objectives were not clear enough for a strategy to be properly developed.

- Audience targeting was instinctive and conventional rather than the result of a scientific and organizationally focused process.
- The messaging and media strategies were never clearly formed from the beginning:

    Message and media choices were based on pure hunches rather than being thoroughly researched in advance among the target audience for credibility, impact, distinction, or ability to achieve the desired objective.

    Decisions were based on too few (and too conventional) choices rather than opening up to the possibilities of unconventional media and message thinking.

- Rather than using quantitative research after pretesting through focus groups, someone decided to develop strategy based on focus group results alone.
- Budgets were based on last year's spending or some other flawed notion. As a result, the resources were insufficient to carry out the strategy, or the strategy could have been executed with a lower level of investment.
- The time frame wasn't properly thought out.
- Strategy was developed with tactics and execution as an afterthought.

How to Strategically Execute Public Relations Tactics

Public relations objectives are achieved through the strategic application of tactics. In the realm of scientific public relations, the heavy emphasis on research comes in the strategy-development stage, but what is learned through that process is applied religiously to the tactical execution of the campaign. Space here is too limited to cover every tactical tool in the PR arsenal, but it's useful to take a quick look at some of the most common, including media releases, spokespeople, media tours and junkets, and special events. Successful use of many of these tools begins with understanding and managing journalist relations.

Journalist Relations

Many of the activities surrounding and supporting tactical public relations are focused on journalists: understanding what they want and providing it to them in a way that advances the PR person's own objectives and strategy. Since that is the case, it is surprising to hear from journalists just how many PR people get it wrong. As stated earlier in describing the Journalist Audit, the attributes that journalists desire most of PR people are *responsiveness* and *access*. This underscores the importance of having a meaningful exchange with every interaction. Delegating unsolicited pitch-calling to junior staffers is a tactic that is almost bound to fail since junior account executives and interns are limited to the very simplest levels of discourse: Did you get the hand-delivered product sample with the complimentary gift basket? . . . Are you planning to run the new product announcement? Nothing bothers journalists more than that—first, because it is a waste of time (they got your gift basket, don't worry), and second because such a call conveys the message that you are relegating the journalist to the B-team (meriting the attention of your second-stringers but not your own attention). And what self-respecting journalist wants this? Instead, when possible, A-list journalists should always have access to your best PR representatives, and the research undertaken during the strategy development stage should indicate which media are the target and which journalists within each medium are most important to your endeavors.

Print, Video, and Radio Press Releases

By the point at which press materials become germane, PR objectives and strategy should be firmly established. When this is the case, press materials deliver the strategic messages to the target media so that they appear in a way that is complete, visible, and positive.

Referring to points made earlier, press materials are most likely to succeed when they represent the interests of the audience you're targeting. Local references to your organization or your brand will make it easier for a journalist to connect your story with local interests, thereby enhancing the likelihood that your story will appear.

One of the most successful media campaigns I've ever seen employed the use of localized press releases for a product sold through dealerships. A limited number of target releases were sent to media within five miles of each dealership and each release was tailored through salient and logical reference to local trends and the local retail outlet. Instead of a headquarters headline with a headquarters city in the dateline, for example, the corporate PR people datelined the story from "Fairfield, Connecticut" and named the local dealership in the headline. The store manager was referenced in the first paragraph with a quote attributed to her. The corporation didn't appear until the third paragraph of the release. While this was a more complicated (and more expensive) process of press release preparation and distribution, the results were astonishing and of extraordinarily high value—a hit rate that cost about 2 percent of that generated by the typical press release. The numbers were unmistakable: a routine press release can be sent over a newswire with an average "hit" rate of 1 or 2 percent of all releases sent. That might amount to a cost of $200 per placement. The localized release cost ten times the least expensive method but the hit rate for this particular example was more than 80 percent of all releases sent, for a per-placement cost of less than $4 per placement—and most of the press releases ran verbatim. In an interesting follow-up, the corporation surveyed the local dealers, 91 percent of whom said that they'd seen their name in the local paper, that customers, friends, and neighbors commented on it, and that new business was attracted as a result of it. More than ninety-six out of a hundred dealers said that they wanted the program to continue. What was more, the program engendered a new category of cooperative marketing: instead of costly co-op advertising support, the company initiated a low-cost and high-value alternative of "co-op PR" that saved millions of dollars.

Photography

Research undertaken for the Impact Score and Net Effect method-ologies cited in Chapter Three indicate that the use of visuals and photos in print and on the air generate awareness and recall levels that outpace stories without visuals. It stands to reason, therefore, that any interaction with the media should be undertaken with visuals in mind. The forethought will be rewarded when larger, more highly controlled and positive stories appear. Conversely, pro-moting different story ideas without the benefit of visual fore-thought will almost assuredly guarantee that your story will appear without a visual asset.

Spokespeople

The CEO as company spokesperson is one of the few no-brainers in public relations, but when it comes time for an outside or celebrity spokesperson, most are chosen on the basis of little more than a gut decision. The process used by a dairy food association to select a celebrity spokesperson showed a more thoughtful approach. Dozens of celebrity attributes were tested for their appeal to the target audi-ence, including gender, source of fame (movies or the athletic field, and so on), and human attributes such as *friendly* or *funny*. After test-ing these attributes through a brief telephone survey, the association had a profile that could be matched against real celebrities. These celebrities were further tested in a second wave of research. The cho-sen celebrity proved to be articulate and comfortable in the role, and competently delivered the association's message despite interview-ers' focus on the reasons for which the celebrity was known (Super Bowl touchdown passes even twenty years after they happened will almost always be more interesting than the sponsor's message). The campaign launched and ran successfully for several years.

Media Tours

The genesis of the media tour is from the day when spokespeople, authors, and movie stars would tour the country for in-person interviews and personal appearances. Nowadays, print and radio interviews can go well via telephone. Television tours, however, are greatly enhanced and essentially require a visual image of the interview subject. These days, television media tours are conducted through the magic of satellite: it's quite common to see your favorite movie star, for example, superimposed on your screen while being beamed in from a remote studio location. As a result of these technological advances, the time and resources consumed in this endeavor have been greatly reduced: the interviewee can conduct twelve personal interviews each hour.

Media tours can be effective, but they run aground if interview bookers focus on the media that they can get or on their clients' irrational compulsion for the "top ten markets" rather than on the right markets for a particular client. (See the sections on the importance of using research to prioritize audiences and target markets earlier in this chapter.)

In one case of a television satellite media tour, a Fortune 500 manufacturer of advanced polymers sought to promote its composites by sponsoring a bicycle design contest in which the entrants were required to use the company's materials. Once the winner was selected, the manufacturer's PR agency went to work on the media tour: "Top twenty markets," they insisted. Not one TV news program in those markets wanted to run the story. The prospect of delivering not a single placement, a fate known in the trade as "an airball," was unattractive, so my firm was asked to deliver a more strategic approach to the media tour. Our first step was to uncover those U.S. markets with the highest concentration of cyclists and our second step was to identify the markets in which the company has major facilities. Both answers were available through inexpensive sources of secondary research (demographics database and Google). The story was pitched anew to target audience markets rather than the biggest markets in terms of general population, and we hit in every market we identified through the scientific process. Granted, the cities in which the story ran were in smaller markets in Montana, South Dakota, and Michigan rather than New York and Los Angeles, but a total of twenty-five top "target audience" markets ran the story, and the client was pleased. It turned out that the PR agency was fixated on the top twenty markets but their client was very pleased that the company could reinforce the superiority of their products among their own employees and among cycling enthusiasts.

Media Junkets

Media junkets involve the transportation of journalists to an exotic location that lends itself to the support of a PR campaign's objectives, all on the sponsor's tab. Unfortunately, according to our research, most elite journalists aren't allowed to accept freebies of this type—and even those who can accept unusual trips don't always consider them particularly important to the development of a story. This may change from industry to industry and from one media outlet to another, but in the case of a cosmetics company that jetted American journalists to an exotic African location to promote their new line of sun protection, journalists themselves later described the trip as a great waste of money. They would have been happier with a much more practical visit to the lab where the new application was developed and a chance to speak with the R&D scientists who helped create it. As part of the Journalist Audit mentioned in Chapter Three, you might consider asking if trips of this type are viable and if they are, what limitations or preferences the journalists have.

Special Events

Special events can be very effective tactics because they can bring visibility to your message and they can be targeted to a particular audience. One particularly memorable and strategic example of a special event was on the U.S. auto show circuit, during which the world's auto companies introduce new models and exciting concept cars. One particular luxury import brand realized that the first show in the four-show season always attracted the greatest attention but also brought with it the most competitive milieu. So the challenge this car maker's PR staff faced was "if everyone is introducing new models, how do we garner attention for our own?" The solution came when they chose to introduce their new model at the third show, New York, rather than the first two. The tactic worked on two levels. First, everyone else had shot their load, so this company owned the show: it captured more media attention at the third show than almost any car manufacturer garnered in the other three combined. And second, they made their pitch in the world's media capital—journalists from around the world had increased access and swarmed the show to get the first glimpse.

Why Tactics Go Wrong

Even the most brilliant strategy can be undone through poor tactical execution. Although a number of things should be considered during your postmortem analysis, you should be aware of the following pitfalls before committing your first dime:

- The strategy was developed without the objectives in mind.
- The strategy was designed without regard to tactics.
- The tactics were created without a firm understanding of the objectives.
- The tactics were undertaken without reflecting the strategy.
- The tactics were created based solely on such dead-end notions as "edginess" or "generating buzz."
- The tactics were undertaken without the target audience in mind.
- The tactics were not designed to be measured or evaluated.

Conclusion

As emphasized at the beginning of this chapter, both strategy and tactics are important. And both need a solid foundation in research. Effective strategies are based on tested theories about how people view your company or product, how they can be persuaded to change their attitudes, and most important, how they can be persuaded to change their behavior. To generate and test such theories takes research. Tactics as well have to home in on the levers of change that research reveals will affect your audiences. In today's competitive and fast-moving world, great hunches are no longer enough (if they ever were). Research provides the key to sound strategy and effective tactics.

Questions Every PR Investment Decision Maker Should Ask

- Does our strategy reflect our objectives?
- Are our approaches to strategy and tactics intertwined?
- Is our target audience clearly defined?
- Is our media list based on the target audience's media consumption habits rather than the agency's Rolodex file?
- Does our messaging strategy take into account what is important to our target audience, how we're performing on what's important, and how our competitors perform on what's important?
- Are our tactics (releases, events, sponsorships) created in support of our strategy?
- Is our entire PR organization engaged in the strategy development before we dispatch anyone to perform tactical activities?
- Were our strategy and our tactics designed to yield a return on investment?
- Do we have a clear understanding of what the measure of success will be?

6

Evaluating Public Relations Programs for Continual Improvement

The evaluation phase for many people is the end of the PR process. A better approach is to see evaluation as simply another step in a cycle that leads eventually to truly refined public relations. In this chapter, we complete the first rotation around the research-based public relations process by examining evaluation—not as an end point but as an ongoing means for managing for continual improvement.

The scientific public relations cycle, which begins with setting objectives and follows with the creation of strategies and tactics, concludes its first revolution with evaluation. At a minimum, the successful completion of the evaluation stage should tell you (and others) how your public relations program performed against objectives and in light of your strategy and tactics. But better still is the type of evaluation that tells you more than just what happened: it tells you *why it happened, if it will continue,* and *what should be done about it.* Let's call this type of research-based evaluation "enlightened evaluation" because it brings with it clarification, illumination, and the context that permits intelligent action. To obtain the extra benefits of enlightened evaluation, you need to put a number of prerequisites in place, as discussed in this chapter.

Evaluation Versus Tabulation

Evaluation in public relations is nothing new. In fact, PR teams around the world do it regularly, even daily if required. However, although public relations is much more than media relations, the most frequently practiced forms of evaluation consist of simple, one-dimensional listings of press clips that do very little to shed light on anything more than who ran a story recently. This type of evaluation is better called *tabulation*, because it is more a matter of typing and rote listings rather than applied intelligence. A surprising amount of resources is expended on this type of evaluation, whether it comes from the hourly billings of a PR agency account executive or in the form of software licensing fees that provide desktop glitz and dashboard glitter (and still require someone to operate the software, interpret the results, and apply them). The worst, one might suppose, is no evaluation at all, but it might be argued that high-cost tabulation is even worse since you're getting little for your money—you're just spending a lot more money to learn little about what your original PR investment yielded. It is common to see weekly activity reports produced by a PR agency's junior account executives showing press releases written, pitch calls made, and news mentions citing the client. This may be fine if the purpose of these reports is to convey productivity rather than outcomes, but it provides little in the way of directional guidance or contextual analysis about what's really being achieved.

To illustrate what passes all too often for evaluation, consider the posting I recently saw for an internship at one of the largest public relations agencies. The internship was for a position producing campaign evaluations for the agency's clients, including some of the world's best-known companies and brands. Considering what could reasonably be expected from a college intern, three things can be inferred about the agency's approach to evaluation: first, since an intern is qualified, the evaluation can't be too demanding; second, the agency is unwilling to produce a level of analysis that might be more meaningful for the client (even if it is beyond the reach of the intern); and third, the agency's clients are almost certainly in the dark about how best to manage their public relations investment intelligently and scientifically as evidenced by their acceptance of intern-level evaluation.

Instead of accepting columns of relatively meaningless media data, executives who invest in public relations should insist upon more consequential and evocative evaluation, ideally comprising a combination of in-depth media analysis and a public relations tracking study (a quantitative survey among the target audience) to ascertain the extent to which a campaign strategy was on target, the degree to which its tactics were effective, and the likelihood that something meaningful might transpire between the organization that funded the PR and its audience.

Public relations evaluation is becoming more and more meaningful as those who invest in PR demand to know more about what has been earned for their investment. Whether the funder is the CEO, the CFO, or the head of marketing, today's clients know that an investment should produce a return, whether that investment is in an acquisition, a new production facility, or an advertising campaign.

For example, the PR staff of one of America's largest financial services companies managed quite nicely, they thought, with what amounted to simple PR tabulation: rows and columns of press clipping data. But other senior executives in the institution were operating under much higher standards: these executives were looking to take public relations further, and along with it, the company. It was their intention to understand the impact of public relations and other forms of marketing on the number of new retail banking accounts opened at their local banks. They created a special interdisciplinary task force to lead the effort. This elite task force rejected the low-level data-gathering system of the current PR administration.

Under protest from the company's PR establishment, the task force chose to evaluate the company's PR efforts using its own method, one better suited for the company's needs. The task force was intent on conducting advanced statistical modeling, which required two years of high-quality PR data to properly represent public relations in an analysis designed to show PR's contribution to sales. Not only was the PR department's existing low-level tabulation unusable for the advanced analysis, the PR leadership was unwilling to alter the approach despite the task force's recommendations. Rather than fighting the conventional PR wisdom, the task force independently—and at some extra cost to the company—chose Delahaye to provide the type of data the advanced analysis needed, which in the end delivered the more sophisticated Impact Score and Net Effect data that helped fuel the task force's advanced statistical analysis.

The task force's efforts were a complete success, considered by the company's C-suite leaders to be among the greatest developments of the year (the case study was a cover story in *Advertising Age*). Among the most important findings was that public relations was much more powerful than previously thought and delivered among the highest volumes of sales for a relatively small investment. Now the task force is seeking to tweak the institution's marketing mix so that even more meaningful results and an even greater return on investment can be achieved through public relations. The organization's chief marketing officer was recently quoted in the *New York Times* as saying that he will direct more resources to PR because of its power to drive sales. Unfortunately, and perhaps one of the greatest ironies in my experience, the public relations department was left out of its greatest victory: it was their programs that contributed to the task force's success, but their stubborn adherence to a flawed evaluation system soured everyone on PR's leadership team. Instead of champions, they were seen as obstructionists. And as the analysis continued to yield exciting new developments over the next eighteen months, the recalcitrant PR leader was further marginalized from the center of excitement until the CEO finally took action and reassigned the job to someone who is both bright and open to new thinking.

What is required for enlightened evaluation—and what is so often missing—is the groundwork that comes well before the evaluation ever takes place, and that serves as the foundation upon which good public relations is based. It's a natural support and continuation of the earlier steps: setting specific, measurable objectives tied to the organization's overall goals and objectives, setting expectations, and getting agreement on the objectives, and then developing strategy and tactics tied to the original objectives. Unfortunately, most people don't do enough during steps one and two for step three to provide much that's meaningful. Perhaps this is because they do not understand the powerful benefits that real evaluation offers.

The Benefits of Evaluation

Enlightened evaluation isn't just numbers, it isn't just a list of activities, and it isn't just a scorecard. The difference between unenlightened and enlightened evaluation is the difference between a report card and a tutor. Here's how:

Evaluation helps decision makers link results to objectives. At the end of the day, your program will have been judged a success or a failure based on the extent to which you accomplished what you said you'd accomplish. This is why it is critically important to set objectives and to get agreement on these objectives right up front: when the time comes to demonstrate how you met or exceeded your objectives, you can draw simple conclusions by comparing objectives with results. In Executive Audit after Executive Audit, we see how some PR investment decision makers—including those in the C-suite—will never be students of public relations, and that may be appropriate for their position. As a result, they evaluate PR performance in one way: Did it meet or exceed objectives? Your evaluation may be a simple checklist that reads "Did it; did it; did it; did it: four for four. This PR program was a remarkable success."

Evaluation provides opportunities for continual improvement. No public relations process, even the most carefully developed, is guaranteed to result in maximum benefit for an organization. There is always room for improvement—and enlightened evaluation provides the means by which successful public relations programs grow even more successful. The best evaluation programs ask questions even as they provide answers. The more you learn, the more you can apply in pursuit of improved results. Human nature dictates that people want to beat the best (until they *become* the best) . . . watch how it takes off among your PR teammates.

Evaluation constructs a framework around which future plans can be built. If your strategy is working, you'll see it through enlightened evaluation. If your strategy is off target, careful evaluation should show you that it isn't working and provide at least some clues as to why. And what you learn in either case can be applied going forward: do more of what worked; do less of what didn't work; refine your own campaign based on what you learn worked or failed to work for competitors. Chances are, if you're following the steps outlined here, your competitors don't evaluate as well as you do. Let them throw good money after bad on strategies destined to fail, while you focus on what's bound to succeed.

Evaluation builds trust. Rather than instilling fear and disrupting work, good evaluation will engage the public relations team and attract them forward rather than prod them. When your intention to launch an enlightened evaluation program is announced, PR team members may be tentative about what may be motivating the change. Many may fear that it will be used as a scorecard and to punish underperformers rather than to give them the means to improve. PR leadership can set the stage by clearly communicating the many good, supportive reasons for initiating enlightened evaluation: it's about making everyone better and enabling the team to produce more effective and efficient public relations programming in the future. Mistakes will be made but they should be viewed as opportunities to learn rather than occasions for punishment. Use and share the evaluation research openly and honestly so that everyone can benefit and grow confident in the process.

Evaluation addresses return on investment and return on expectation. When everything is said and done, it is reasonable to expect the evaluation to tell you whether you received your money's worth when compared to past performance and when weighed against other forms of marketing and communication. Even if you can't attribute expenditure to sales or some behavioral measure, you can use media content analysis to attribute a cost-per-impression or cost-per-thousand reached (with positive, potent news coverage) when evaluating a media campaign. An analysis of relative cost efficiency is preferable and within reach when no absolute cost analysis is possible. In terms of *return on expectation*, which was first discussed in Chapter Two, remember the importance of demonstrating *value* as defined by those who are funding the program: Did they get the results they expected? This is a useful means of proving value when no absolute measure such as sales is available or appropriate.

The "Evaluation Benefits" sidebar on p. 142 summarizes the benefits of enlightened evaluation.

Evaluation Research Tools

Public relations evaluation employs the same research tools discussed in Chapter Three for the objectives-setting and strategy-development process applied thus far: content analysis of news coverage, quantitative surveys, and statistical modeling for the purposes of evaluating outputs, outcomes, and business results. In this case, however, these research tools are being applied to the goal of assessing and understanding the degree to which your public relations program succeeded or fell short, why it succeeded or fell short, and what should be done in light of what you've learned. Sometimes evidence of success is only indirect, as in surveys of consumer attitudes and how they've changed. But in other cases research can provide direct evidence: for instance, if the PR campaign is designed to reduce the presence of pollutants in local streams (as in the Falmouth example discussed later in this chapter), surveys and content analysis may not be as meaningful or direct as testing the actual level of pollution before the campaign and after.

Surveys for Enlightened Evaluation

The application of survey research in evaluation is the same as the research used prior to setting objectives. At this stage, the goal is to assess the current landscape and how it has changed as a result of the PR program (as well as other potential variables). Because you already know your priorities as they relate to target audience identification, media prioritization, and message engineering, you need only a small investment of resources to develop the necessary findings.

Typically, the evaluation stage employs tracking surveys to assess the extent to which people are aware of the campaign, brand, or organization; understand it; and intend to act now that they know what they know. Tracking can be continuous or intermittent. Continuous evaluation gives you a consistent and reliable source of incoming intelligence rather than waiting for the end of the program. On the other hand, intermittent evaluation is less expensive, and it may be all that you need. Most serious, measurement-based public relations programs use a pre- and a post-campaign survey to establish levels of awareness and understanding that can be compared.

Evaluation Benefits

Enlightened evaluation is critical for a number of fundamental reasons:

- To clearly demonstrate a positive return on investment
    Generating sales
    Doing more with less
    Avoiding cost
- To verify that the objectives and strategy were properly set
- To identify shortfalls which need to be addressed
- To refine future strategies to generate an even better ROI
- To secure resources and funding

Those who invest in a public relations campaign expect that it will go beyond generating media coverage to engender positive attitudes and deliver some level of understanding, preference, or behavior among the target audience. Evaluation surveys should tell you the extent to which your key messages are remembered and the degree to which the brand messages are imprinted in people's minds. You also hope to ensure that the messages people associate with the campaign were the ones you intended to deliver. Awareness is assessed through open-ended questioning to which respondents give unprompted responses. Recall in isolation does not automatically correlate with impact in the form of behavioral change, so awareness measurement looks to assess both specific messages and also a larger attitude or inclination to support or do business with you. If your target audience free-associates positive attitudes toward your brand, then you can assume that the intended messages are creating a positive environment for behavioral change. Awareness, of course, is only a means to an end. It is more important to show that people who are aware exhibit attitudes or behaviors more supportive than those of people who are not aware.

A PR campaign conducted for the town of Falmouth, Massachusetts, provides a good use of survey research for evaluation. Falmouth was facing a serious problem with nitrogen pollution in its bays and ponds. As much as 15 percent of the nitrogen pollution, which caused rapid algae growth and fish kill, was coming from the chemical fertilizers residents put on their lawns. O'Sullivan Communications was hired to launch an educational campaign to inform Falmouth residents about the problem.

Before the campaign was launched, a benchmark survey was executed by survey maven Annette Arno to learn more about the target audience and their understanding of the issue. The survey revealed that most residents had a comprehensive understanding of the nitrogen-loading problem and believed it needed to be addressed. As a result, O'Sullivan chose to focus campaign resources on educating residents about solutions to the problem instead of creating an issue awareness campaign. (This preliminary survey research was critical to the success of the Falmouth program. Had the team just picked an obvious target such as "raising awareness," the campaign would not have been a good use of limited resources since residents were already aware.) After an educational campaign that included direct mail, public relations, and community outreach programs, a follow-up survey of 6,500 residents attempted to determine the effectiveness of the campaign. The results showed the following:

- 82 percent of respondents agreed with the statement, "I can help reduce nitrogen pollution by adopting a Falmouth Friendly Lawn."

- 80 percent of Falmouth residents surveyed agreed with the statement, "Nitrogen pollution from chemical lawn fertilizers is a serious problem for Falmouth's bays and ponds." (Up 10 percent from the precampaign survey.)

- A clear majority of survey respondents rated the brochures, postcards, newsletters, and newspaper articles as effective (3.73 on a 1–5 scale, with "5" being "very effective") in providing helpful information.

- 49 percent of the people surveyed now indicated that they fertilize their lawn in the spring and fall only, the fertilization schedule promoted in the campaign.

- Falmouth's bays and ponds improved as a direct result of the campaign and, coincidentally, sales of nitrogen-healthy organic fertilizer nearly doubled in all local garden centers.

Beyond survey research that focuses on the attitudes and behavior of the target audience, the Journalist Audit and Executive Audit can also provide useful insight during the evaluation phase.

Journalist Audit. For those PR professionals who focus on media relations, it is important to assess the degree to which journalists come to know your campaign as well as your PR department and agency as a reliable source. The Journalist Audit script used during the evaluation stage is identical to the one used prior to the campaign. The Journalist Audit should be conducted once each year to make sure that the program is on track with the expectations and preferences of key journalists. (See sample Journalist Audit in Appendix 3.)

Executive Audit. Like the Journalist Audit, the Executive Audit should be conducted on an annual basis to reveal any changes in the organization's business priorities as well as the latest opinions of those who invest in PR. What is more, it has been our experience that certain industries tend to have high rates of turnover—think brand managers at consumer-goods companies—so it is important to constantly refresh one's PR perspective by adding the opinions of any executives who have joined the organization since the last audit. The questionnaire will change only fractionally, if at all, from year to year. (See sample Executive Audit in Appendix 1.)

Media Content Analysis for Enlightened Evaluation

The content analysis used for evaluation is usually a smaller-scale version of the content analysis done during the planning stage, usually because the planning stage content analysis can go back a year or more and the ongoing evaluation is done on a monthly or quarterly basis. The goal remains assessment of the quantity and quality of media coverage by target audience, by media outlet, by intended and unintended message, by journalist, and so on across competitors and over time.

Target Audience Reach. The target audience will have been identified during the planning stages of setting objectives, and its media preferences will have been identified as well. Target audience reach is concerned with reaching the *right* audience rather than just a big audience. Some executives who invest in PR may have been trained to expect bigger numbers than target audience reach may provide; if so, you should explain that this is an important distinction that extends the organization's public relations resources significantly. PR campaigns cannot dictate what stories the media will choose to run, so if the general audience greatly outweighs the target-audience reach, it may simply be that your story has a broader appeal than just among your target audience. If your release was picked up over the Associated Press or the NBC Network news feed, hundreds or even thousands of media outlets will have access to your story with permission to run it locally (and it doesn't cost you an extra penny). That's not a bad thing, but you should be able to assess whether or not good resources were put against reaching secondary and tertiary audiences when you'd have gotten a better response from a more focused approach. Look at your target audience results versus your own past performance to judge whether things are headed in the right direction. Also look at how your competitors performed in these media to see whether they might be succeeding in ways that were not part of your original objectives and strategy. If you can mimic their strategy among these media or leapfrog them, you'll have neutralized any advantage they might have and you might surpass them.

Volume of Coverage Among Target Media.   Along with target audience identification, research-based PR concentrates on specific media based on the media habits and preferences of the target audience. Enlightened evaluation will focus on the target media identified at the outset of the campaign and assess the extent to which coverage was generated in the targeted media. Look at past performance as well as the performance of your competitors to determine if any underachievement came as a result of your strategy and tactics or whether it might be an issue related to your industry category.

Use what you learn to revise your target media objectives, if necessary, and review strategy and tactics to improve your target media penetration and distinguish your positioning among competitors over time. Suppose you have generated coverage among "important, high-penetration media." If your organization generates a higher quantity of higher-quality coverage than any competitor, then the suggested action is "keep it up" or "continue to build on your strength." If your organization generates a higher quantity of lower-quality coverage than your competitors among preferred media, then the suggested action is "fix it—fast." If you generate a comparable volume of high-quality coverage, then you must "maintain," or you will otherwise cede a strong position of parity. In those cases where you generate a comparatively low volume of lower-quality coverage among preferred media, then you have an opportunity: if you can be the one organization to positively differentiate yourself versus competitors among these important media, you will have earned a position of real strength.

Following through on "less important media," you also find four segments for action: If you generate a higher volume of higher-quality news coverage among *less* important media, you have a dual opportunity: you can either sell up the importance of these media to your program, or you can review these results as a possible over-investment and decide whether to cut back. If you generate a comparable volume of higher-quantity and higher-quality coverage in less important media, it's generally best to maintain or cut back— don't put additional resources against these media. And finally, if you are underperforming on less important media, then our advice is to keep the status quo: don't invest further (after all, these media don't matter to your target audience). Table 6.1 illustrates a sample target media analysis. It breaks out media outlets by name, volume of coverage received by the sponsor's brand and its competitors, and an evaluation of the overall tone of the story.

Key Message Delivery. At the beginning of the scientific public relations process, specific messages are identified as the most credible and most compelling means to communicate the organization's position. The enlightened evaluation should be able to tell you exactly how these messages performed in terms of the frequency, tone, and positioning of the messages as well as how the messages performed alongside one another. Ongoing evaluation will uncover the extent to which the quality of your key message delivery evolved over time and against competitors. If the evaluation indicates that your messages are underperforming, try to uncover the cause either through content analysis or by surveying journalists: it could be that the messaging strategy is on target but your tactics are off-center, or maybe your spokespeople aren't properly focused. These tactical missteps are correctable; it is much worse to discover at this stage that your messages are not considered either compelling to your target journalists or believable coming from your organization. If your messages are performing at or above your initial expectations, reinforce your efforts to increase your margin of victory.

Table 6.1. Target Media Analysis.

	Client			Best Competitor			Average		
	Positive	Negative	Total	Positive	Negative	Total	Positive	Negative	Total
Daily Newspapers									
USA Today	1	0	1	8	1	9	3	1	4
New York Times	44 □	5 ○	49	14	0	14	6	1	7
Washington Post	18	1	19	17	2	19	11	2	13
Wall Street Journal	59 □	1	60	4	1	5	2	1	3
Chicago Tribune	33	2	35	39	1	40	24	3	27
Broadcast									
ABC	19	4 ○	23	45	12	57	27	4	31
CBS	20	6 ○	26	22	3	25	14	2	16
NBC	2	0	2	3	1	4	1	1	2
CNN	33	3	36	36	6	42	22	7	29
Auto Enthusiast Magazines									
Car and Driver	21 □	3	24	12	2	14	6	2	8
Road & Track	11	1	12	17	1	18	8	1	9
Motor Trend	2 ○	1	3	24	0	24	13	1	14
News and Consumer Magazines									
Time	3	1	4	4	2	5	2	1	3
Popular Mechanics	6	0	6	7	0	7	2	0	2
US News & World Report	1	0	1	4	1	5	1	1	2
Business Press									
Forbes	6	2	8	12	2	14	6	2	8
Crain's Detroit Business	16	4	20	22	4	26	18	6	24

Key: ○ = Fix; □ = Reinforce

You should follow the strategy adjustment framework discussed for the volume of coverage in target media based on your analysis of key message delivery. For example, in the case of the messages that your target audience considers to be "important," decide whether your strategy going forward should be "keep it up," "fix it," "maintain it," or "look for opportunities." Follow an analogous process with less important messages to decide whether to "sell up," "cut back," or "maintain." Table 6.2 illustrates this sort of message analysis in action.

Unintended Message Delivery. As a result of your carefully set objectives and the wisdom of your strategy, most of the messages you deliver will be those you intended to deliver. But sometimes, especially if you are in an organization that is regulated, under scrutiny,

Table 6.2. Message Analysis: Number of Stories Carrying Key Messages with a Positive Tone.

Car Attributes	Client	Best Competitor	Average
Acceleration	56	123	33
Attractive and Stylish	92 3rd	140	41
Comfort	76	153	49
Environment	16	113	22
Fuel Efficiency	(4)	79	14
Handling	34	101	25
Innovative and Advanced Technology	239 4th	341	108
Layout of Controls	21	23	8
Price and Value	112 2nd	205	57
Quality	45 5th	90	24
Reliability	27	39	13
Ride	12	42	12
Safety	51	71	19
Utility	31 3rd	176	43

Key: □ = Top 5 (Rank); ○ = Key Weakness

or otherwise highly visible, some of the media coverage your organization produces will be unexpected or at least off-plan. Unintended news coverage can be unflattering or negative. Nonetheless, it is important to track unintended messages because they can be an early warning of worse things to come. If the messages are negative and inaccurate, you need to educate, but if the messages are negative and accurate, you may have bigger problems. You may wish to accelerate your evaluation schedule for weekly or even daily reporting if the negative news smells like a crisis in the making. Use the evaluation to focus your attention on balancing the unintended messages with intended (positive) messages. One pharmaceutical company we know tracked a drug recall on a daily basis and managed the negative news about this product with healthy doses of positive news about the overall corporation's progress on diversity and other areas of corporate and social responsibility. The lasting effect of the negative stories was almost certainly greater than that of the positive stories, but the impact of the negativity was offset by the company's ability to demonstrate its vitality and long-term focus.

Unintended news coverage isn't necessarily a bad thing: a competitor's dramatic loss of market share will almost certainly point journalists in your direction. Hopefully, you'll be able to show how your market share is stable or improving. When Sears and Kmart merged, for example, a lot of attention was shifted toward Wal-Mart. Wal-Mart's only involvement in the story was that the Kmart–Sears merger was attributed by analysts to what the merged companies had to do to compete with Wal-Mart's market supremacy. This perspective, which played over and over again in the media, worked in favor of Wal-Mart.

Journalist Trends.   Content analysis should tell you something about the reporting tendencies of your target journalists. While the Journalist Audit will reveal how journalists feel about your organization, your brand, or your campaign, the Media Content Analysis will tell you how journalists report on your organization, your brand,

and your campaign. Combine what you learn from both exercises before drawing conclusions, and then reach out directly to journalists to clarify your message and answer questions that might arise. Some Delahaye clients have taken our research directly to the journalist and shared it so that meaningful and mutually beneficial dialogue could take place.

Spokespeople and Third-Party Citations. Enlightened media evaluation tells you more than just what reporters are saying: it also tracks who is influencing the reporters and what the influencers are saying. Journalists often use third-party industry and financial analysts to add perspective to their reporting. In recent years, the powers of industry analysts such as those from Gartner and Forrester have spawned a whole new category of public relations known as *analyst relations*. But outside analysts are not the only ones shaping news coverage: your organization's own spokespeople have a great deal of influence, too. The media evaluation should track spokespeople, analysts, and other opinion leaders by name and by the themes represented through their commentary. Use the media analysis to track outside sources and their commentary toward your organization and your competitors or opposition. Determine whether any bias exists. Whether you see bias or not, do what you can to make sure they know what they need to about your organization in order to provide (even more) positive commentary. Negative commentators may warrant your outreach or your avoidance, depending on what you know about them. Internal spokespeople can be difficult to manage despite the vested interests you share in putting the organization in the best of all possible lights, but you should be able to track the frequency, tone, and content of their citations to help them measure how they're doing and how they might be able to improve. Discuss their personal results with them privately and consult with them so that their performance can be reinforced or improved, depending on what you learn. A whole business is devoted to training executives, celebrities, and sports stars to interact more effectively with the media, and you may need to bring in out-side help.

Tactics Tracking. Much of the resources that are ultimately spent during a public relations campaign will be spent on media tac-tics, the activities and events that drive media coverage. So it only makes sense that enlightened evaluation will track the absolute and relative performance of each tactic. Press releases, special events, media tours, and promotional tie-ins can all be measured in terms of their ability to generate attention within target media, to pro-duce positive treatment of your key messages, and to generally im-prove the return on your investment in public relations. You ought to be able to see any trends in terms of which media covered the tactic and which didn't, which covered competitors and not you, and which ignored you and your competitors. Determine which media deserve your attention in the future and which ones you need to understand better going forward.

Impact Score. Chapter Three introduced a distilled scoring system called the Impact Score and Net Effect, which has been proven to correlate with meaningful business outcomes such as sales. The Impact Score is derived from the physical characteristics of the news item—use of visuals, placement in the headline, and exclusivity, among others. Enlightened evaluation provides you with measures for each impact component so that you can improve your scores going forward. While behavioral outcomes rather than high Impact Scores are the end game, we've seen so many cases where high Impact Scores correlate with awareness and behavior that they can serve as an interim objective. When you have re-ceived your Impact Score results, compare your results against those of your competitors and against your own past performance. And, most important, compare them to your objectives to ensure that you are on track while there's time to refine the program. Assess why your program performed as it did regardless of whether you met or fell short of expectations. There's always room for improvement.

Guidelines for Effective Evaluation

If you invest in public relations, you should demand enlightened evaluation; if you provide PR services to internal or external clients, they deserve the benefits of enlightened evaluation. Here's how to get the best out of your evaluation system:

Evaluate consistently and frequently rather than opportunistically or just at the end of the campaign. Because the world is a place of constant change, a strategy that is successful today may not work well in the future; evaluation that is recurrent and unswerving provides a solid benchmark for program tweaks to be made intelligently and as quickly as required. Too often, evaluation is undertaken only at the end of the program or after the program has ended. We've seen enough people scrambling to "revisit the numbers" and other acts of last-ditch desperation when it's too late to make a difference. The best evaluation provides insight along the way so that if an unexpected shortfall occurs, you have both the time and the directional guidance to make the proper adjustments before the end of the campaign. Recalibrations and corrections are made throughout so that the final weeks of the campaign are filled with confidence.

Ensure that your evaluation provides understanding. It is worth remembering that the less management knows about anything—including, and maybe especially, public relations—the more they will rely on data . . . but data only tells part of the story. For this reason, the evaluation should offer executives within and outside the PR department a degree of comprehension that data alone cannot. What can be made of the PR evaluation that provides only numbers without perspective? So what if you generated 1,321 stories? Was that good or bad? How did your competitors perform? Is there room for improvement? Who cares if your awareness levels improved by 10 percent if sales are down? Answers to these questions are not impossible to provide, and these answers can engender deep levels of understanding and intense appreciation. And it's important to remember that you can hit your targets and still lose the battle if you don't add context and understanding to your evaluation.

Make your evaluation precise. Public relations is considered by some to be a "soft science," which is to say that they regard PR as difficult or impossible to measure. Don't add to their suspicions by providing vague, inaccurate, or inflated data. When conducting media relations evaluations, use only audited circulation and verified broadcast and Internet audience data. At all costs, avoid the use of so-called multipliers, which serve only to distort the numbers by inflating them. And if practicable, avoid advertising equivalency; PR and advertising are distinct, and ad values oftentimes underrepresent the value of PR. (See the sidebar: "Beware of Multipliers and Advertising Equivalency Measures.") What is more, anyone with experience in buying advertising knows that the rate-card rates are almost never paid at retail. Why undermine your performance by introducing debatable measures? And what of the PR people who evaluate performance in terms of "significant media coverage" or "major gains in media awareness" without the aid of specific data to support the claim? They run the risk of being misunderstood, undervalued, and marginalized when the conversation turns to generating a serious ROI. If you're evaluating awareness, you should use the same awareness measurement techniques as others within the company; consider piggy-backing on their research so that the relationship between different initiatives can be crystal clear.

Beware of Multipliers and Advertising Equivalency Measures

Two forms of PR measurement are highly debated and questionable: the first is the use of a *PR multiplier,* wherein circulation or ad value is factored or multiplied by an arbitrary number to reflect the added impact of PR, and the second is the use of an *advertising equivalency measure*, wherein a dollar figure is applied to news coverage on an "if-purchased" basis.

PR Multipliers

Users of PR multipliers inflate circulation or audience (or equivalent advertising value) by a certain factor designed to track the alleged real impact of the message. Factors ranging from 2.6 to 7.3 have been reported. When program results are presented, data are reflected in terms of both the actual circulation or audience along-side impressions, which is the term frequently used to represent the factored or post-multiplier circulation or audience figure.

Those who use and advocate the use of PR multipliers base their argument on two foundations:

- *Pass-along rates*. These rates are based on the idea that more than one person reads each newspaper or magazine purchased, and therefore, straight circulation and audience figures undercount the actual reach of the news item.
- *PR value*. This multiplier relies on the premise that public relations is more credible and carries more impact than advertising and therefore deserves a higher weight than straight circulation and audience.

The assumption, and it is a risky one, is that these factors are used consistently, repeatedly, and quantifiably. They are not, and there lies the danger.

While public relations has been proven to carry demon-strably more impact than advertising *in some cases*, and while every public relations professional has a vested interest in elevating public relations within the corporate and marketing communications mix, the practice of using PR multipliers comes with considerable risk and should be avoided. Here are four real-life scenarios where the use of multipliers is hazardous:

- The marketing client uses more than one PR agency, and each agency uses a different multiplier. The resulting differences in the reports cause confusion and undermine confidence.
- The brand manager is an experienced advertiser and insists on seeing the (nonexistent) underlying research that details just how much more impact PR carries than advertising.
- The agency client compares notes with another of the agency's clients and discovers that different account groups use different multipliers.

Continues

- The product manager replaces one agency with another, which uses PR multipliers and has to defend the radical increase over the prior agency when there were no new or significant PR initiatives.

Recommendation

Take advantage of the best, most consistent, most reliable, and most easily defendable media data. Given the availability and widespread acceptance of audited circulations for newspapers and magazines, Arbitron data for radio, and Nielsen data for television, there is no credible way or reason to factor the data.

The use of pure circulation or audience data is the safest way to ensure that program results can be confidently reported and supported on a program-to-program, company-to-company, country-to-country, and year-to-year basis.

Ad Values

Searching for a way to demonstrate public relations results in terms of a dollar value, many PR people equate public relations in the form of news coverage to the cost of buying an equivalent amount of advertising.

Among ad value advocates, the argument is that space in a newspaper or time on the TV news can be purchased, and since a publicity placement occupies time and space in the same way that advertising does, the amount of money that one would have to spend on the equivalent advertising purchase can be reasonably applied to the placement.

The equating of public relations and advertising in this way is risky for a number of reasons:

It assumes that PR's internal clients don't know how advertising differs from PR. Typically, PR raises funding from marketers, and marketers know a lot more about how advertising is purchased than most PR people do. The key difference is that advertising buyers (also called advertising or media planners) aggressively negotiate lower rates through package deals, bundling, long-term commitments, and other measures, while those who advocate the use of ad values in PR use the highest possible rate, otherwise known as the *rate-card rate*. Advertising planners who actually bought space or time for the rates PR people use in their comparisons would be out on their ears before they knew what hit them.

Users of ad value equivalents also assume that PR holds an equal value. In other words, the assumption is that one dollar's worth of advertising space is equal to one dollar of PR. As mentioned in Chapter One and reaffirmed throughout this book, public relations often delivers results *far better* than a dollar's worth of advertising. Why undervalue your work? Equating PR to a dollar value can be sexy (unless, of course, the ad value is too low), the information is easily attainable, and probably most important, PR clients don't insist on better methods—but none of these reasons hold water.

The use of ad values inevitably leads to the pursuit of higher ad-value media outlets rather than of a higher quality of media placement. As noted in Chapter Three, it is quite common to find that the most appropriate media targets are often those outside major market areas. A local newspaper may have a higher-quality audience reach and lots of other advantages, but the ad value is less than $10 per column inch. By contrast, generating coverage in *People Magazine* may equal a far higher ad value, even though it does not reach nearly as high a concentration of the most valuable audience segment.

Ad value assumes that PR and advertising are the same, which they are not. Using ad values to measure PR undermines what it is that makes PR unique in the marketing and communications mix. PR professionals should be champions of and for public relations rather than blurring the lines of what differentiates PR from every other form of marketing communication: credibility, audience engagement, and low cost for high value.

Recommendation

PR professionals should refrain from using ad values (and beware of ad values disguised by other names). To be fair, I have seen serious PR evaluation undertaken where ad value correlates with other, more meaningful outcomes, but evaluations comparing ad value to sales or other measures of business performance are

Continues

extraordinarily rare. Most ad value proponents show the dollar figure and leave it at that. If advertising value is viewed in terms of what drives higher ad values—a publication with high circulation or a prestigious and essential industry newsletter combined with a large, dedicated amount of space or time—then a higher ad value indeed can be a positive reflection of the quality of placement (this is how proponents of "media value" position their argument). And in relative terms, generating a higher ad value this month than last month may be a good thing if everything else is accounted for. In my experience, however, many alternatives offer lower risk, and these should be considered as the primary avenues to measure public relations effectiveness.

Make sure your evaluation is relevant. Pertinent evaluation tells you, those who work for you, and those to whom you report how you're doing against the measures that matter. Imagine the PR person who reports to management in terms of clip volume when the most highly regarded measure is "awareness." Chapter Three discussed the Executive Audit, a qualitative research instrument by which you can assess the expectations of people who are investing in your public relations program. Report back in those terms—but remember that the measure most often cited among executives who invest in public relations is simply *whether it met or exceeded the objective*.

For years, executives at one of the world's great technology companies grew increasingly anesthetized to their public relations because of irrelevant tabulation. Then the PR department began reporting the results of the company's most respected competitors as part of their own evaluation reports. When these same executives saw that their competitors were consistently performing at levels greater than their own, the results became extraordinarily relevant, having tapped into the deeper motivation of competition. Beyond tracking media coverage, this PR department added a survey component to its evaluation so that everyone knew what changes were taking place in the minds of the target audience.

Reflect externally driven changes in your evaluation where appropriate. No public relations campaign exists in a vacuum. It is common to find that results have been affected by external events that have nothing to do with the campaign itself. For example, in the news media, events such as the Michael Jackson trial or Hurricane Katrina will practically close the news window for as long as the event is newsworthy. For months after the 9/11 tragedy, news programs rightly devoted extraordinary amounts of their resources to focus on this national crisis. Many tried-and-true forms of public relations such as publicity stunts and other inane but ordinarily acceptable forms of generating visibility were not considered appropriate in the post-9/11 environment. It doesn't take a national tragedy to upset the balance, but enlightened evaluation provides an outwardly focused view of what external events might have affected the PR campaign.

Indicate the effect of internally focused events and strategies. External events aren't the only factors that can affect the performance of a public relations campaign. We've seen corporate earnings announcements undermine a new product launch, and we've seen what appeared to be an isolated brand-related event affect future launches for years to come. Organizations are often so large and so decentralized that the marketing and communication of one division can actually conflict with another's. We've seen advertising campaigns that promote trust and value competing against PR on behalf of the same brand emphasizing service and loyalty. While PR pushing one theme when advertising pushes another doesn't necessarily spell disaster, such efforts can be harmonized for a greater overall impact. Ideally, an organization's communication and marketing strategies are synchronized well before the evaluation stage of the scientific public relations process, but it doesn't always happen, especially among different departments. The best evaluation includes a glimpse at what else was occurring within the organization during the public relations campaign that might have had either a positive or negative effect on the PR outcome. During the evaluation process, it can be useful to compare results on a pre and post basis, using control group research to help uncover negative or positive performance gaps.

Managing the Evaluation Process

So far, this chapter has focused on evaluation tools and methods. Just as important as using the right tools and methods is managing the process wisely. The choices you make about evaluation providers, budgets, and other matters can undermine the whole process. Here are my recommendations for managing the evaluation process:

If at all possible, make sure the evaluation is performed by an objective third party. To ensure an unbiased evaluation, entrust the process to people outside the organization who have no vested interest in reaching a positive outcome, just as you hire third-party accounting firms to come in to audit the books. Unfortunately, most organizations have their agencies evaluate their own work, which is an untenable situation. "Trust me" shouldn't cut it when so much is at stake, and besides, your PR team ought to focus on what they do best: generating great public relations results.

Find the best research company you can afford based on methods, quality of analysis, integrity of data, and strength of the organization, in terms of both people and financials. If one proves its mettle, stick with it. If you change research providers every year or two, the evaluation data may not be consistent or even comparable. Seemingly small differences in methodology (media analysis tone ratings using a scale of 1–3 versus those using a scale of 1–5, for example) will almost always destroy data comparability.

Commit to evaluation even if it takes time and resources. Traditionally, one of the first cuts during a downturn is public relations, and among the first things cut from the PR budget are research and evaluation. But when resources are tight, that's the time to make sure that your expenditures are being properly channeled toward those PR strategies and tactics that are tested and later validated to yield the desired result. Scale back? Maybe. Eradicate? Foolish.

Evaluate even if some aspects of public relations are difficult to evaluate. Sure, it's hard to measure "the effectiveness of good counsel" or "a crisis avoided," but this is no reason to throw the baby out with the bathwater. Enlightened evaluation will provide you with a great deal of insight on most PR activities and functions, and in those cases where a direct measure is difficult, indirect measures are plentiful.

Invest in evaluation over the long haul even if evaluation may sometimes capture only short-term results. If your public relations programs are more tactical and project-oriented, your evaluation routine may only provide for project evaluation rather than ongoing analysis. Make sure that your evaluation program is the consistent, overarching measure by which all PR programs—long- and short-term, strategic and tactical—are measured.

Make sure that the evaluation connects with the people who funded the PR. The key to successful evaluation is the creation of objectives that are meaningful, measurable, and reasonable, and that come with sign-off from your sponsors. The most direct way to connect with your investors is to provide evaluation that links to the original objectives and initial expectations. Use terms that are clear and precise.

Take advantage of an integrated, comprehensive system. Smart companies conduct media analysis and survey research to get the most out of their evaluation programs; smarter companies make sure that both modes are assimilated with one another and with other forms of marketing and corporate communication research to gain even greater intelligence.

Use your evaluation as a learning tool. Sure, you want every program to succeed, but that doesn't mean that future programs can't be even more successful. Similarly, even underperforming public relations programs provide a basis for learning. Those who limit their evaluation to score-keeping efforts miss enormous opportunities for continual improvement. Embrace underperforming programs, however painful, so that mistakes are never made again.

Use consistent methods. Some large organizations use more than one public relations agency, and different agencies have different methods. This is a sure way to make certain that you learn nothing from one campaign to the next as you choose different agencies for different campaigns. Insist on a consistent method and make sure it's the one you endorse.

Conclusion

When it comes to evaluating public relations, some organizations are content to amass piles of data, which provides little illumination. A more enlightened approach is to use research to consistently and continuously measure the effectiveness of your program, not just to justify your tactics. Analyzing the results of your public relations program can provide information that will lead to a better program next year—and even better results.

Media content analysis, surveys of journalist and executive opinion, and awareness tracking are only a means to an end. Whenever possible, show the interconnectedness of the process: journalists who have good experiences with your PR team are more likely to promote your position, and media who cover your position favorably are likely to make people aware of your organization and what it represents. People who are aware of your organization and what it stands for will exhibit more supportive attitudes or behaviors than those not aware. Supportive behavior promotes positive business results.

Time will tell, of course. When evaluating PR programs, remember that success may build slowly, but it is certainly contingent upon intelligence, consistency, and continuity. The results of the evaluation process sometimes suggest changes in your strategies or tactics, but changes should be made carefully and cautiously. Over time, your annual program evaluations will help you tailor your public relations program for maximum effectiveness and efficiency.

If you consistently pursue the keys to successful public relations, preliminary research, research-based objectives, research-based strategy and tactics, and enlightened evaluation, you will gradually increase the yield from your PR investments.

Questions Every PR Investment Decision Maker Should Ask

- Did we meet or exceed our objectives?
- Did we outperform our competitors?
- Did we reach our target audiences?
- Did we deliver our key messages? Did any unintended messages appear?
- Did our target media respond?
- How have we changed?
- How has the competitive environment changed?
- Has the target audience done what it was supposed to do?
- Did those with awareness do more of what we want than those not aware?
- Are we generating a positive ROI? Is our PR leading to sales, lowering costs, or avoiding costs altogether?
- Will these trends continue?
- Did PR meet or exceed relative efficiency within the marketing and communications mix?
- What worked and what didn't?
- Did we gather the feedback we need to improve?
- How can we do better?
- What do we do next?

Part Three

TRANSFORMING YOUR PUBLIC RELATIONS PROGRAM

7

Real Business Results

Proving—and *Improving*—PR ROI

The benefits derived from scientific public relations extend far beyond simple efficiencies and improved effectiveness: millions—and even billions—of dollars are in play. Ideally, the methodical approach to public relations outlined in earlier chapters leads to meaningful business results, that is, a measurable contribution to the organization by generating revenue, lowering costs associated with superior performance, or protecting against threats to the company. This chapter explores these three hallmarks of PR power using real-life examples to illustrate each one.

Using Public Relations to Generate Revenue

The easiest way to make a connection between PR and sales is by assessing the contribution of PR when it is used in isolation, as the only form of marketing in operation. When nothing else is going on except for PR efforts, then it is safe to say that PR is driving any increase in sales. For example, when a certain frozen foods company celebrated the fiftieth anniversary of its pioneering brand of frozen entrees, it did so with just a modest publicity campaign and no special advertising or promotions. Within the anniversary month, the publicity generated a 40 percent sales boost in the overall frozen entree category and an even greater increase for the anniversary-celebrating brand. In this case, the only required research tool was a simple clip tabulation of generated stories and sales data against which the clipping data were compared. When there is no other effort present, it can be that simple. When it's possible to do, this is still the fastest and most inexpensive approach to tying PR to sales.

However, few companies use PR in isolation, without other marketing agents, and until recently, that meant that it was rarely possible to isolate or measure PR's contribution with any rigor at all. Now, the convergence of new technology, advanced PR measurement, and superior statistical methods enables marketing analysts to connect a variety of activities with their impact on sales. As a result of these developments, known collectively as marketing mix modeling, the impact of any particular marketing agent on sales volume can be quantified even when concurrent marketing activity and other external factors are present. Armed with this new understanding of what works, marketing investment decision makers can devote their dollars to the areas where they are known to do the most good.

Marketing Mix Modeling

Marketing mix modeling, which was described in Chapter Three, is growing in popularity but it is generally focused on those marketing agents with the biggest budgets—meaning that it tends to exclude PR. The main hurdle in undertaking marketing mix modeling is assembling and organizing the data. That being said, if the company sponsoring the statistical modeling has been measuring marketing and communication properly and consistently, the data that feed most marketing mix models are relatively simple: frequency and reach of advertising or direct marketing, also known as "Gross Rating Points" or GRPs, segmented by market and within a given time frame. For PR to be properly represented in the model, one must have the data that best integrate into the model and best represent what makes PR unique in the mix. Chapter Three introduced news content analysis, and Chapter Six detailed how content analysis is used for evaluation. Content analysis evaluation data enrich the marketing mix analysis by representing PR: frequency, reach, Impact Score, and tone, collectively known as the "Net

Effect" segmented by topic, over time, and within target markets. By following the recommendations in this book, especially in Chapters Four through Six, you can generate PR results that can be incorporated into the model so that the value of public relations becomes impossible to overlook.

In dozens of cases from categories as diverse as long-distance telephone service to beer to movie tickets to financial services and automobiles and consumer goods, traditional and online retailing, marketing mix modeling proves that PR is capable of delivering among the best ROI of anything tested. Case studies featuring actual brands are extraordinarily hard to find as the elite organizations benefiting from this approach consider it to be top secret and prefer to keep their secret advantages, well, *secret* from competitors. In this chapter, we're fortunate to be able to document several such cases.

Making the PR-to-Sales Connection at Procter & Gamble

With seventeen brands with sales over $1 billion apiece, overall sales exceeding $57 billion, and an advertising expenditure of almost $6 billion annually, Procter & Gamble is widely recognized as one of the world's greatest marketing organizations. Given the extent of the company's significant global marketing investment, marketers are tasked with generating the optimal return, preferably in terms that clearly demonstrate a direct and meaningful contribution to sales. In common with those at other companies, P&G's marketers face complex challenges:

- How much volume and profit does each marketing agent contribute to my business?
- What is the ROI of each marketing driver?
- How should my budget be allocated across the marketing mix to optimize profits?
- Which tactics increase volume and profit most effectively?
- Is consumer response varying over time?
- Are there synergistic effects across my marketing efforts?

P&G marketers in advertising, promotions, and trade measure their performance using research and evaluation methods unique to their discipline. To maximize the company's *overall* marketing investment and to provide answers to the challenges listed here, P&G employs marketing mix modeling. In this way, P&G has led the way with new and traditional marketing approaches under the umbrella of holistic, consumer-centric marketing based on *what works* rather than conventional wisdom. However, public relations performance had not been broadly or consistently integrated into P&G's marketing mix analysis. Then in 2005 P&G decided it needed to establish public relations into its marketing mix modeling to quantify not only the extent to which PR promotes awareness of the company brands but also the degree to which PR drives sales. Given the amount of simultaneous marketing expenditure across the globe, this was no small undertaking.

With the full support of P&G marketing and under the leadership of P&G's External Relations executive Hans Bender, it was agreed that public relations data would be fed into preexisting marketing mix models to learn more about just how public relations initiatives contribute to sales, both in PR terms and in relation to other marketing agents. By verifying the process by which P&G could link PR to sales, the company's marketers and the PR people who support them would be able to improve PR efficiency and effectiveness, create public relations strategies pretested to deliver sales, and integrate PR analytics into the brand planning process as a key element of improving overall marketing—not just PR–ROI. Once this process was established, it was branded internally as "PRevaluate," and the plan was to expand the program globally across all P&G brands.

For more than a decade, Procter & Gamble has collaborated with Delahaye, the company's primary public relations research and evaluation partner, to accurately assess performance and to provide research-based guidance for P&G's PR-based "Influencer Marketing" (IM) programs. The objective in taking this approach is to accurately, consistently, and affordably represent the uniqueness of IM programs within the marketing mix and to clearly demonstrate PR's contribution to sales by brand, by product, by campaign, and by media type over time and across regions. In so doing, the goal was to provide P&G brand marketing investment decision makers with the reliable intelligence they need to efficiently boost sales volume. The research program targeted the conventional marketing wisdom within P&G, where marketers trusted the value of PR but lacked sufficient basis for making a quantifiable connection between PR and sales.

Public relations performance data were assembled from 2003 and 2004 for seven pilot brands, including Olay and Pantene, as well as the brands with which they compete. Print, broadcast, and Internet coverage was evaluated for the presence of specific components such as frequency, reach, tone, and key message delivery. Each brand's media coverage was also analyzed based on reach, frequency, and quality of coverage. From the complete set of data, P&G's marketing mix modeling team identified certain elements to use as the basis for properly representing the unique qualities of PR within the marketing mix model.

To prove the PR-to-sales connection, enormous amounts of data, including week-to-week sales and marketing data from around the world for each brand, were gathered, integrated, and analyzed. PR campaign plans, tactics, and results for a total of seven brands were mapped across a time frame of from one to three years, and the resulting data were assembled and analyzed. The sales, marketing, and PR data were subsequently processed through the marketing mix analysis to determine the outcome.

The marketing mix analysis results proved positive: PR-based Influencer Marketing was shown to efficiently deliver high levels of return, often surpassing the ROI of mass-market advertising, price promotions, and trade activity. As a result of this endeavor, P&G has made measurement an integral part of all major IM programs on key brands globally. The expectation is that PR's new measurement focus will likely drive a higher degree of discipline throughout PR, and that measurement will allow for consistent learning, recycling, and application. Remarkably, this project required no incremental spending; it was simply an advanced application of preexisting research and analysis endeavors. Figure 7.1 illustrates the differential spending on PR and other forms of promotion at P&G.

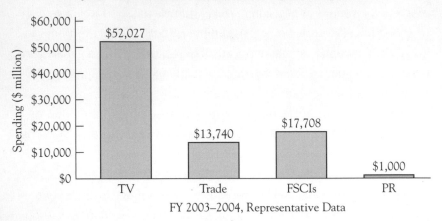

Figure 7.1. P&G Promotional Spending Data.

FY 2003–2004, Representative Data

How PR Lifts Other Forms of Marketing

Given industry prognosticators' forecasts for increased levels of marketing communications spending—TV and print advertising alone constitute hundreds of billions of dollars worldwide—marketers are challenged to show how—and whether—this extraordinary investment generates a positive return. And further, how do the separate forms of marketing communication interrelate? And if a positive relationship exists, how can it be leveraged to create even more effective and more efficient communications programs? Until 1998, little had been done to understand whether and how public relations interacted with other forms of communication.

The AT&T Study

To return to the example presented at the beginning of Chapter One, as one of the single largest investors in marketing and corporate communications during its day (prior to the merger with and rebranding of SBC), AT&T had a vested interest in leveraging its marketing and communication resources for the greatest possible return. As a first step in understanding and generating a positive return on the company's total communications investment, AT&T's public relations research guru Bruce Jeffries-Fox invited Delahaye and the NPD Group to work together on this groundbreaking project. Delahaye was the company's media relations research provider, and the NPD Group was its advertising tracking research provider. For more than a year, Delahaye's senior VP Wayne Bullock, the firm's most sage research expert, served on this multidisciplinary team, which sought to explore and uncover the truth about how advertising and PR interact in affecting customer preference and loyalty, which in the world of long-distance telephony constitute the bottom line.

The task was made more difficult since AT&T's PR and advertising, as in most large organizations, were managed in silos by different departments, often employing their own agencies, and were measured using different methodologies. Finally, AT&T's advertising and PR were constant and concurrent, so teasing out their respective contributions to customer perceptions, attitudes, and behavior was particularly challenging.

Two sets of preexisting research were used in this exercise. Because complete sets of annual data were required, 1997 was chosen as the benchmark for further study. The first set of research came from AT&T's Ad.Visor Advertising Effectiveness Study, conducted by the NPD Group, which used telephone surveys to track the degree of loyalty AT&T engendered among its customers. The study segmented customers into the categories of *Real Loyals, Moderate Loyals,* and *Vulnerables.* The survey also tracked the extent to which AT&T delivered on certain attributes, including *Trust* and *Value.* Through statistical analysis, advertising frequency and reach (GRPs) were compared to loyalty and perception measures. Through the survey data analysis for any given level of advertising, AT&T was able to predict loyalty and perception scores.

The second set of research data came from the media content analysis that Delahaye had provided. The media content analysis analyzed a broad array of both general and specialized news coverage, including print and broadcast media. The system tracked a number of factors related to news coverage beyond just the content and the tone of the story. The Impact Score, which has been referenced throughout this book, was developed with AT&T and Bruce Jeffries-Fox in the run-up to this initiative.

Since the AT&T advertising tracking research continuously measured advertising recognition and loyalty every two weeks, Bullock's media analysis team also reviewed media results in two-week increments. Spikes in coverage (illustrated in Figures 7.2 and 7.3) helped identify AT&T's biggest positive and negative stories of 1997. Among the biggest events, two stood apart:

- *President's Summit on Volunteerism:* This conference promoting volunteerism garnered widespread positive media coverage for sponsor AT&T. The event featured every living past U.S. president, as well as luminaries and business leaders including AT&T's leader at the time, CEO Robert Allen.
- *"Dialing for Dollars":* In late 1996 AT&T brought to market a simplified pricing plan which provided "One Rate" for all calls at all times. However, in early 1997 many news stories appeared citing

Figure 7.2. Predicted versus Actual Loyalty (News Coverage Favorable).

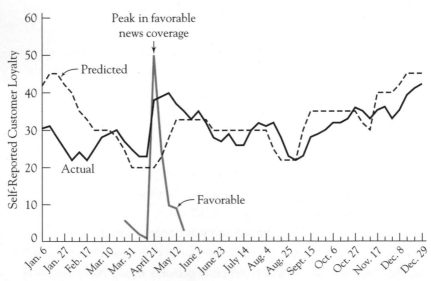

Figure 7.3. Predicted versus Actual Loyalty (News Coverage Unfavorable).

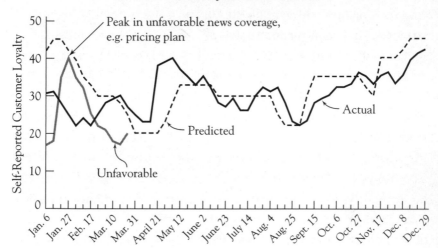

cases where individuals were quoted different prices. *60 Minutes* ran a very visible, very credible negative story and in the weeks that followed, negative articles presented AT&T as being less than forthright with consumers.

Under Bruce Jeffries-Fox's leadership, the research team took AT&T loyalty scores and attributes-ratings (trust and price/value) during the two-week period of each news story, adjusted them for advertising weight levels, and compared them to average scores for the year.

In this way, AT&T was able to identify the impact of good and bad news on customer loyalty in light of heavy and light advertising. Jeffries-Fox hypothesized that the *Volunteerism* event, with its enormous number of positive, high-quality media impressions concerning AT&T, would boost AT&T loyalty measures, and that the opposite would occur with the *Dialing for Dollars* event, given the large amount of negative media coverage aimed at AT&T.

Over time, the survey-based analysis became a marketing mix analysis, where the findings reaffirmed what every PR professional believes but has had so much difficulty proving: proactive, positive public relations has the power to boost customer loyalty *even in the face of reduced ad spending,* and reactive PR yielding negative news coverage can hurt customer loyalty *even in the face of increased ad spending.* That negative news coverage can overwhelm advertising in some situations surprised AT&T's advertising people, who might have attributed decreased loyalty scores to ineffective advertising.

Beyond the implications for public relations specifically, the study demonstrated the importance of PR's role within the overall marketing mix: heavy ad spending won't be fully optimized without a proactive PR contribution. Further, a relatively light ad spend can be more fully leveraged through the effective application of proactive public relations, an important consideration for companies unable to afford heavy mass-market advertising. In other words, good PR makes other forms of marketing more effective in a way that no other form of marketing could approach.

Finally, the results dispelled the myth that PR's ROI can only be shown when it works in isolation, without the presence of alternative forms of marketing communications. In fact, PR can clearly demonstrate its impact even when advertising is present and constant.

This program resulted in many shared awards for AT&T and Delahaye. In the years that followed and right up until company divisions were divested, AT&T continued to gather insights aimed at demonstrating—and generating—a positive return on public relations investment.

How PR Drives Sales

In the December 2003 issue of *TelevisionWeek*, renowned marketing journalist Joe Mandese reported how the Miller Brewing Company, one of the nation's largest marketers, changed its marketing strategy, shifting budgets out of TV advertising and into public relations. Miller's marketing team learned that PR has a significant impact on actual product sales relative to other forms of marketing, especially TV advertising (see Figure 7.4). Mandese quoted Ranjit

Figure 7.4. PR's Impact on Beer Sales.

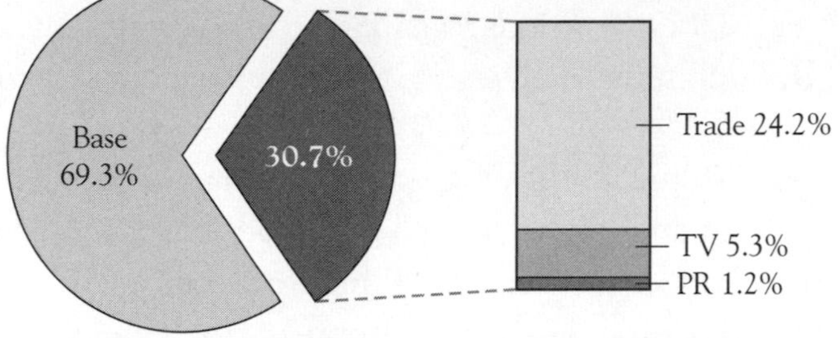

Choudhary, the marketing mix modeling specialist for Miller at the time, who said, "In this study we found out that PR was much more efficient than other promotions for the brand." While their findings warranted further research, which had not been done at the time of the interview, Mr. Choudhary predicted a change in Miller's marketing mix and that the change would come "at the expense of TV advertising budgets that would be shifted into PR."

While more and more major marketers conduct the type of modeling discussed by Choudhary, extraordinarily few track or reveal the impact of PR on sales or its impact relative to other forms of marketing. But for Miller, which based its analysis on two and a half years of data—including sales, promotional spending, ratings from Nielsen Media Research, and proprietary PR research provided by Delahaye, the marketer uncovered PR's contribution to the bottom line. For example, as shown in Figure 7.4 and based on their analysis, Miller learned that its PR campaigns generate roughly 1.2 percent of base product sales or 4 percent of incremental product sales. That may not seem like a lot, but TV advertising was attributed with only 5.3 percent of base sales and 17.3 percent of incremental sales. While Miller's precise advertising-to-PR spending ratio was not revealed in the article, it should be noted that the U.S. industry average is estimated at 61:1 in favor of ad spending. Assuming that Miller's ratio is similar, its PR was approximately 15 times more efficient than its advertising.

Figure 7.5 shows the relative efficiency of additional spending on various forms of marketing. Trade advertising brings a return of roughly $2.20 for every dollar spent, and TV advertising delivers $1.06. PR, by contrast, delivers $8, the best of any marketing agent tested.

Armed with the intelligence derived from marketing mix modeling, PR programs can be created based on what's most likely to drive sales. The bar chart shown in Figure 7.6 shows the sales impact of three PR programs versus "impressions," one of PR's more conventional and less revelatory measures. If you had the choice to invest your resources in campaigns like number one, two, or three, which would you choose? Campaign one drove impressions, so for most traditional PR practitioners, that looks like the sure winner on the surface. But dig deeper and you see that campaigns two and three efficiently delivered a remarkable sales yield through relatively small impression counts. If you're beginning to think like me, your money is on these two campaigns,

To learn more about marketing mix modeling within your organization, ask people in marketing and market research and they

Figure 7.5. Efficiency: Incremental Spending and Revenue.

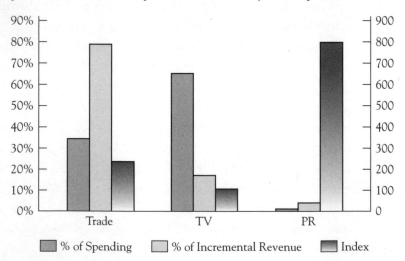

% of Spending   % of Incremental Revenue   Index

Figure 7.6. Volume per Million Impressions.

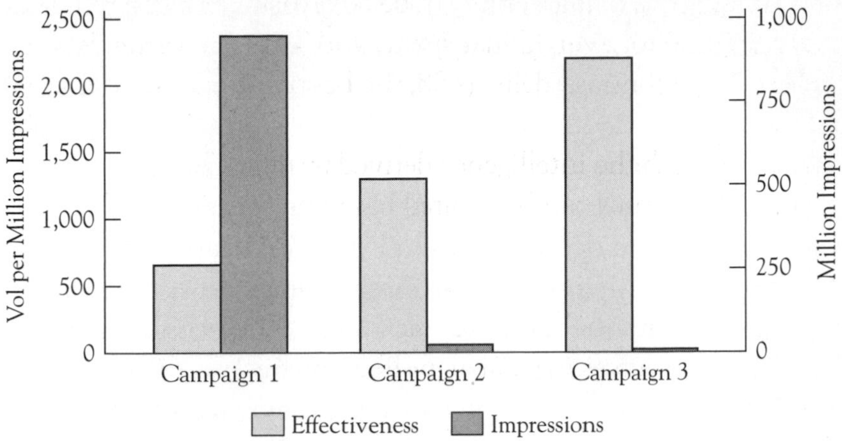

may be able to guide you. Chances are that you will have to initiate this quest for yourself as most marketing mix modelers do not know enough about PR to seek you out. The price of entry is two years of public relations data including the Impact Score and Net Effect (or some other distilled score of PR performance) broken out by key market and on a week-to-week basis. If you don't have this information readily available, your media analysis provider can use on-line databases to retrieve two years of historical content for further analysis before feeding it to the marketing mix modelers and as long as the content you can uncover matches the key market area media being fed into the model (local newspaper coverage, for example, may be impossible to retrieve).

Doing More with Less

PR professionals work diligently every day to deliver better results within the limitations of their budgets, but few seem to recognize that this is an ROI equation contributing directly to meaningful business results. Simple examples such as using targeted media lists for press release distribution, repurposing your digitized video for easy journalist access via The NewsMarket or using your video news release audio for a radio news release may seem small but they can add up. Figure 7.7, which represents the number of wire releases distributed by the hundred largest U.S.-based corporations as tracked in the Delahaye Index of Corporate Reputation, shows that some companies generate a higher-than-average volume of news coverage even though they distribute an average number of releases. The circled data point in the figure indicates a company that generates a very high return on its releases, while the one in the square indicates a company with a low return. Most companies fall into the category of "normative failure"; the dots bunched in the lower left represent those who don't spend enough to break from the pack.

This phenomenon plays out in many industries. For example, a retailer once used a rigorous public relations measurement program to test the worth of an annual brand-sponsored fishing tournament designed to support the company's line of fishing gear. It turned out that the event generated very little media coverage, which prompted the brand PR executive to probe further, at which point he discovered that the net profits for this particular sporting goods line were less than the cost of the sponsorship. The exec returned hundreds of thousands of dollars to the company's coffers by simply "doing more

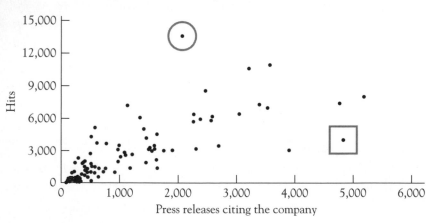

Figure 7.7. Doing More with Less.

with less and for less." The several millions of dollars that were saved were available to aid the company's bottom line or to reinvest in a more worthwhile form of PR or marketing.

Confirming the Hunch: Using Research to Identify Areas of Improvement

Founded in 1991, Ipswitch is a small, private developer of Windows-based software products that enhance the productivity of users from consumers to IT professionals. It competes with some of the giants of the software industry in the messaging and network management markets and is the leader in the file transfer protocol (FTP) market space with its product WS_FTP Pro.

The public relations department of Ipswitch regularly interacts with journalists regarding a range of corporate and product issues and relies on this form of marketing to position its products in a positive light to potential and existing customers. However, Ipswitch felt there was room for improvement in its U.S. and U.K. programs. Ipswitch wanted to determine how successful it was in getting its messages across to journalists so that in turn they would relay these messages to their audiences.

It decided to survey the influencers—the journalists themselves in both countries—to better understand what they knew about Ipswitch and its products.

Nearly two hundred journalists from the United States and United Kingdom were contacted using a custom survey research instrument. Eighty-one interviews were completed (more than 41 percent of the entire sample): twenty-eight with U.S. contacts and fifty-three with U.K. contacts.

The Journalist Audit confirmed the hunch. Many journalists, particularly those in the United Kingdom, cited a low level of familiarity with Ipswitch and its products. However, the good news was that those who reported familiarity with Ipswitch reported a high perception of the company, its products, and its PR department.

Based on the findings, Ipswitch decided to address these short-falls in the following ways:

- *Increase the frequency of and investment in press tours.* Ipswitch had averaged one press tour per year in Europe, centered around product releases. It now proposed to conduct two European press tours and one U.S. press tour annually with IT and business publications regardless of product release announcements.

- *Conduct an Ipswitch press event.* To generate visibility and a sense of newsworthiness, Ipswitch decided that an annual Ipswitch press event featuring its president, Roger Green, could provide industry overviews and outline the state of small business or IT-related topics.

- *Position Ipswitch as being responsive to customers.* Ipswitch promoted its customer service orientation by publicizing customer events (such as customer user meetings) and pub-lishing more case studies highlighting customers' use of Ipswitch products.

Using research to pinpoint the areas where it was strong and where it was weak allowed Ipswitch to make the most out of the PR budget and get the best results from its tactics.

Doing More for Less and with Less: Six Sigma

New methodologies and technology are being integrated to foster the science of public relations and to ensure optimized public rela-tions performance. One of the most important emerging forms of this integration is Six Sigma, a quality and performance philosophy originating at Motorola and now under way at many of the world's leading companies.

Six Sigma is a disciplined, data-driven approach and method-ology for eliminating defects (or deviation). The term itself is derived from statistics, whereby one tracks "defects per million opportunities" in terms of *sigma* (the name of the Greek letter used in statistics as a symbol for standard deviation). In this case, a *defect* is described as anything outside customer expectations. By definition, Six Sigma is less than 3.4 defects per million, or a success rate of 99.9997 percent. Given that most companies perform at a two-to-three sigma level (roughly 70 percent to 93 percent), a four sigma level or 99.38 percent success rate sounds pretty good (it would mean a solid "A" in school). But it also means that 6,210 of every million airline flights would have something go wrong, potentially ending in disaster.

Essentially, the purpose of Six Sigma is to gain breakthrough knowledge on how to improve processes to do things better, faster, and at lower cost. It can be used to improve every facet of business, from production to human resources to technical support and, yes, even public relations and corporate communications. Unlike some other quality improvement efforts, some of which may have been the latest fad at *your* organization, Six Sigma is designed to provide tangible business results, which is to say, cost savings that are directly traceable to the bottom line.

Approaching PR in this methodical fashion—even if it isn't at Six Sigma levels—forces you to be more focused in your thinking and by so doing, improve the value of your public relations. At its core, Six Sigma revolves around a few key concepts, each of which can be related to everyday PR decisions:

- *Critical to quality:* Attributes most important to the customer
- *Defect:* Failing to deliver what the customer wants
- *Process capability:* What your process can deliver
- *Variation:* What the customer sees and feels
- *Stable operations:* Ensuring consistent, predictable processes to improve what the customer sees and feels

The Six Sigma process begins by first understanding who your internal and external customers are (in PR, internal customers are those people who fund PR; external customers might be journalists, analysts, employees, and customers). Second, but no less important, comes understanding the needs of customers so that customer expectations can be met. Tools that are commonly used in the process are surveys, focus groups, and customer panels, and since many of PR's internal clients are looking for media coverage, content analysis of news coverage may be critical in satisfying them.

In the late 1980s, Work-Out was the start of GE's quality management journey. As Dave Ulrich, Steve Kerr, and Ron Ashkenas describe in *The GE Work-Out* (2002), GE used the program to create a culture open to ideas from everyone and everywhere, cutting back on bureaucracy, and making boundaryless behavior a reflexive, natural part of the GE culture. This created the learning environment that led to Six Sigma. Today, Six Sigma in turn has embedded quality thinking—process thinking—across every level and in every operation of the company.

While Six Sigma's customer-focused, data-driven philosophy has been applied throughout GE, it had not been consistently applied to communications functions within the organization. The GE Corporate Communications team was convinced it could use the Six Sigma quality process to improve PR execution and ensure that media coverage always met or exceeded the target effectiveness and productivity measurements.

Beginning in 2000, GE and its research partner, Delahaye, began to test, refine, and verify how the measurement data Delahaye compiled for the company on a monthly and quarterly basis—particularly Delahaye's Weighted Impact and Net Effect methodology—could be applied toward the Six Sigma process. Later that year, GE began the initial series of Six Sigma analysis projects that continued into mid-2001. The business objective was to develop a real-time strategy for consistently improving and controlling overall PR productivity (costs), ROI, and effectiveness in reaching and influencing GE's target consumer, customer, and investor audience segments.

One measure of PR effectiveness that was used in the Six Sigma process was key message penetration. Once the company identified its five most important messages, PR staff could look at the messages as they actually played in the media and see where they missed. The process looks like this:

1. *Define:* Identify meaningful elements that can be measured consistently.
2. *Measure:* Apply metrics against the measurable variables.
3. *Analyze data for defects:* Isolate cases where, for example, stories appeared without the elements defined as *meaningful*.
4. *Find root cause:* Look at how you communicate; look at how journalists receive your communication.
5. *Put improvements in place:* Make sure that all communication contains the key message and that it is delivered in the way that journalists prefer.
6. *Institutionalize 100 percent:* Once you've undertaken the process, make the corrected process the standard.

The objectives of GE's initial Six Sigma analyses were to identify and then control the independent variables influencing their Weighted Impact Scores (quality and quantity of news coverage) and production of positive media impressions. By understanding which factors they can control, PR staff would be able to focus their efforts on driving these factors to ensure optimum media performance and PR productivity.

Based on its Six Sigma experience, GE developed a PR Effectiveness Control Plan that was used in its PR efforts, including media relations strategy (media relationship management, media mix targeting), product exposure strategy (product exposure guidelines), and overall resource allocation. These efforts ensured a closer alignment of PR objectives with the strategies and business goals of the organization. Research findings verified that the business impact is significant:

- A substantial improvement in overall PR productivity (activity performance per dollar spent)

- A 16 percent decrease in "cost per positive media impression" produced
- An 8 basis-point increase in the number of positive media impressions produced
- A 20 basis-point decrease in the number of negative media impressions produced

The GE Corporate Communications team was the first of any PR team at any company we know to have attained Six Sigma certification.

As you consider how you might bridge public relations and Six Sigma, keep in mind that, typically, PR and corporate communications do not take the lead in Six Sigma programs. So while you may have metric systems to contribute, you may have to go in search of your organization's Six Sigma leaders. Also, since Six Sigma metrics lend themselves to projects, there are a number of projects you can undertake (see sidebar, "Six Sigma Project Ideas for PR") within or outside a formal Six Sigma environment.

Six Sigma Project Ideas for PR

- Reduce time for press release approval.
- Improve media targeting (identify media that have proven reach among your target audience).
- Assess journalist preferences and satisfaction with current PR initiatives.
- Assess internal client preferences and satisfaction with current PR initiatives.
- Improve the ratio of releases sent to releases used.
- Improve the ratio of placements featuring key messages.
- Improve the ratio of placements featuring a company spokesperson.
- Improve the ratio of stories featuring visuals or graphics.
- Improve the ratio of stories that are feature-length exclusives.
- Improve the ROI of events and event sponsorships.
- For agencies, improve percentage of billable hours.

While Six Sigma and public relations are new partners, the application of research and PR continues to grow as companies demand to know how their money is spent and how it can be spent more wisely. Six Sigma has met with such enormous success that it is unlikely to be just the latest business fad. Put simply, the organizations that prevail will be those that find the right data, analyze the data accurately, and apply what they learn.

Protecting Against Costly Threats

In the case of "doing more with less," the amount of money to be saved is limited by the PR budget. In dealing with threats to a company, the stakes are much, much higher, as good public relations can be related to sums in the billions, especially in its role as protector of corporate reputation. Consider these recent events:

- The Bridgestone/Firestone and Ford crises caused market-value drops of more than 50 percent.
- Johnson & Johnson's Tylenol tampering caused a $1 billion (14 percent) drop in market value.
- Intel's Pentium chip crisis caused a $3 billion (12 percent) market value drop.

It should come as no surprise that companies with a good reputation enjoy benefits over companies without it. In 1992, Oxford University conducted studies to chart the impact of man-made catastrophes on the market values of fifteen companies. The "reputable" stocks sagged only 5 percent in the first few weeks while the "non-reputable" stocks lost 11 percent. After ten weeks, the "reputables" rose to a net gain of 5 percent, where they remained. The "less-reputables" languished below the levels they enjoyed before the catastrophe.

Effective PR can protect companies even when the bad news is relatively routine and nonspectacular. When TXU, a leading Texas-based power utility, knew it would fall short of its quarterly earnings estimates in 2002, its senior management weighed the pros and cons of the "head-first" versus "no-comment" approach. PR leadership urged CEO Erle Nye to act on research that showed distinct media patterns: a proactive approach correlated positively with a shorter period of negative news coverage, whereas media coverage tended to be protracted when the organization was less forthcoming. Coincidentally, the news trends tracked consistently with share price: when companies got out in front of the issue, the stock price (like the tone of news coverage) took a short dip and then returned to normal—whereas the ostrich approach tracked with a more severe and sustained stock-price decline. CEO Nye took no chances and followed the advice of his PR team. The company saw a negative spike on the first day and some residual interest for another day or two, but the story quickly died. During the first twelve days, TXU averaged a modestly positive "+18" using Delahaye's Net Effect Score, a distilled number for assessing the quantity and quality of news coverage where a "0" is a strictly neutral rating. By the end of the quarter, TXU ranked second among twenty-six American power utilities whose media coverage is tracked in Delahaye's syndicated Power Brands Report.

Three other energy-related firms, Reliant, Dynegy, and Duke, faced earnings difficulties of their own in 2002. Whether it was by design or not, the leadership of these companies was slower to respond. Coupled with other issues, their media coverage (and coincidentally, their stock price) suffered as a result. Using the Delahaye Net Effect Score again to track the first twelve days from when the potentially negative news broke, Reliant's average score was –39.6, Duke generated an average score of –74.2, and Dynegy's average score was a whopping –251.6.

Stopping the Big Grab: Keeping Banks Out of Real Estate

In 2001, the Federal Reserve drafted a regulation allowing federally chartered banks to enter real estate brokerage and property management, businesses from which they have been barred since the 1930s.

The ramifications of the rule were tremendous. Mega banks could control the entire real estate transaction, with potential conflicts of interest when brokering and financing the same deal, limiting consumer choice. The impact to America's hundreds of thousands of real estate agents would have been catastrophic.

Insiders believed that the chances for stopping or slowing the proposed rule were remote, but the National Association of Realtors (NAR) knew that the rule could change forever the way Americans buy and sell homes. NAR decided to mount an all-out effort to delay and stop the rule. In 2001, NAR conducted surveys and focus groups among Realtors and consumers. Findings confirmed that consumers supported NAR's position, and the feedback fine-tuned messages that had been used in the first phase for a print and radio advertising campaign that broke in early 2002. Following the attitudinal research, NAR conducted an analysis of its media coverage as specifically related to the banking issue.

- Key findings indicated that NAR owned more than two-thirds of the exposure on this issue in 2002 and dominated the American Bankers Association (ABA) for share of all positive exposure— coverage that favorably represented the organization's position— with 86 percent.
- In addition to dominating the level of coverage in the top publications contributing stories, NAR bested ABA in terms of positive stories, notably in *American Banker,* where half of NAR's stories were positive compared to only 8 percent for ABA.
- Thirty-eight percent of NAR's articles communicated one or both of the specific banking issue messages, which bested ABA's average level of message communication, which was 17 percent of all articles for 2002.

By gaining a handle on which messages were resonating in the media, NAR was able to determine the efficiency of its public relations efforts, provide a perspective on media results relative to communications priorities and legislation, and develop new public relations specifically tailored to meet the findings of the study.

More than four years have passed since the rule was promulgated and it has yet to be implemented. This has never happened before in recent history. As a result of the NAR's communications efforts, the Federal Reserve received more public comment on this rule than on any other in its history. In response, a majority of the members of the House and Senate who had sponsored related legislation abandoned their support, and Treasury Secretary O'Neill withdrew the rule from consideration in light of the overwhelming opposition among members of Congress and the public. On February 14, 2003, Congress passed legislation denying funding for implementing the rule, thus killing it for the near future and sending a clear message to regulators that the proposal was against congressional intent.

Conclusion

The days when PR could depend on a clip-book to represent ROI or value-for-money-spent are over: these case studies prove that the return on investment of public relations is quantifiable and, when done properly, can contribute toward the organization's overall business goals and objectives.

Questions Every PR Investment Decision Maker Should Ask

- Does our organization measure the ROI of public relations programs?

- Does our organization plan PR programs with a measurable ROI as an objective?

- Does our public relations research provide us with a road map for improvement?

- To what extent does our PR contribute to sales? Provide better results for less money? Avoid costs altogether?

8

From Concept to Reality

The marketing and corporate communications of the past are going the way of the dinosaur. But just as the dinosaurs' extinction fueled the world's evolution, so too is it true for our profession: public relations is a prime beneficiary of the changes under way. PR is enjoying a new beginning within many organizations as more communications investment decision makers come to recognize the ability of PR to deliver credible and involving messages relatively inexpensively and with high impact. As a result, PR professionals are being asked to meet increased levels of accountability (which is good) and subjected to a greater intensity of scrutiny (which is sometimes unpleasant), both of which require us to prove our ability to deliver a positive ROI.

An informal survey among a gathering of a hundred professional communicators attending the 2004 IABC/Delahaye Research and Measurement Conference in New York yielded interesting findings that point to the challenges and opportunities PR practitioners now face throughout the profession. Communicators know that they must contribute a positive ROI, yet they don't have systems to assess ROI. PR's internal clients expect and are provided formal objectives from their own management, yet PR measurement systems able to assess the extent to which a particular PR objective has been met have not been broadly implemented.

This chapter sketches the highlights of the reported trends, why they're happening, and what you can do about them.

• *Nearly nine out of ten strongly agreed with this proposition: "My company's communications program objectives are tied to business objectives."*

Just as every other area within the organization has been required to demonstrate a measurable contribution to business goals, so too is this now true for PR. In most organizations, public relations is among the last departments to be held accountable, but this is changing, as demonstrated by this response. *Business objectives*, of course, can mean different things in different organizations, but it almost certainly means delivering results that are meaningful, measurable, and, if you're lucky, reasonable.

• *Only five out of ten agreed with this proposition: "My communications program objectives are measurable."*

If you were building a transcontinental railroad, wouldn't you want the tracks in alignment when they met in Utah? This response is the PR equivalent of a train wreck, but it is surprisingly common. Each year, Delahaye interviews roughly a thousand senior executives who have some level of control over PR spending, in an effort to help PR pros align their programs with their companies'. In every case, the executives demand objectives that are measurable, meaningful, and reasonable—or it's back to the drawing board. For half of the respondents to openly agree that their objectives are not measurable is a form of serious self-admitted malpractice.

• *Virtually all respondents (96 percent) agree with this proposition: "Top management is aware of my communications program objectives."*

Each year, Delahaye conducts survey interviews among PR people attending professional development events. Year after year, we hear that generating press clipping volume is the *most common* and *most meaningful* goal for a successful PR program. And year after year, PR's internal clients say that press clipping volume is the least important measure of all. That top managers are *aware* of your objectives doesn't mean that they *support* them. Senior execs would much prefer to see programs that *deliver messages to target audiences, raise awareness, change attitudes*, and finally, *affect behavior*.

Given the number of disconnects between PR staff and the bill-paying management, it's natural to look for reasons—and, once again, our mini-survey provides an illustrative answer:

- *Six out of ten respondents allocate 3 percent or less toward measuring their PR programs. Almost four out of six of those (36 percent of the total) spend 1 percent or less.*

A variety of interested parties recommend that a fixed figure of 10 percent of the total PR budget is appropriate, year in and year out. But that is not a desirable course; whether it's 10 percent or 2 percent, the PR budget and the research budget should not be in lock-step: expenditures should vary with the organization's needs at a given time. For example, a mature brand with a huge PR budget may require only a fraction of 1 percent whereas a category-redefining significant new product roll-out may justify spending 10 percent or more during the initial phases. If your organization has no experience with PR research and needs to conduct a benchmark assessment of its PR environment, develop a message and media strategy, and identify potential spokespeople within a specified time period, it will require a significant investment. But once the initial investment is made, it may require only marginal investment in subsequent years to monitor the program. The biggest obstacle is often not one of dollars but of managerial support, and managerial support is more likely to be gained if the appeal is made in the language of business than in traditional PR-speak.

- *Nearly four out of ten use "anecdotal observations" or have "no program in place to measure ROI."*

Given that more and more organizations are looking for PR to contribute to business objectives, they need some kind of systematic and reliable level of accountability to accomplish this. Anecdotes won't cut it and having no way to measure PR's contribution is professional suicide in the current environment. I remember the new EVP of corporate communications for one of the world's ten largest companies: he proudly told me that his only measure for PR performance was the comments he attracted on the executive corridor, and that he didn't need to quantify or justify his programs. Last I heard, he's out of PR and working as a novelist, a field in which anecdotes really are the stuff from which success is born.

- *Four out of ten respondents believe that the biggest issue facing PR today is "credibility/trust." Almost three out of ten say it's "proving ROI."*

These challenges are inextricably linked: how can PR engender credibility and trust within the organization if it cannot prove how it delivers?

The people who participated in this mini-study should know: 90 percent have worked in public relations for more than five years and more than half have been active for ten years or more. Almost 80 percent of the respondents would be considered management-level and above. In terms of the organizations represented, 65 percent were corporate, 17 percent agency, 13 percent nonprofit, and 4 percent came from government offices.

Clearly, measurement is one of the most critical challenges facing the public relations profession. The need has been identified and methods have been developed, many of which are available to those with even the smallest budgets. So why don't more PR people use research and evaluation to set objectives, develop strategy, and improve performance over time? Professionals express a number of concerns.

Overcoming Objections to Research

PR people have many reasons (or excuses) for not doing research. Listed are some of the more common objections to doing research, along with my responses.

- *The costs will outweigh the benefits. What will we find that we didn't already know?*

Sure, a level of investment is required to undertake a serious and rigorous public relations research program. But the better question might be, What is the cost of not proving and improving your value when your competitors are proving and improving theirs? Chapter Seven included a number of examples of how PR research delivered a positive return on the research itself. If you could avoid a billion-dollar market-cap drop or if you could add millions of dollars in sales in exchange for spending $30,000 for research to provide the required guidance, the question wouldn't be "Why do it?" but "How often can I do it?" and "How soon can I get started?"

And as for only being able to learn what you already know, it is true that research often reflects your hunches. But there is value in validating what you know because even if your PR victory is obvious to you, it may not be obvious to those funding your PR programs. And you never know what you might learn that is surprising and transformative.

• *This will be a lot of work for senior management: setting research criteria and measurement definitions, selling it, and so on.*

It's true that instituting a research-based public relations program can be time-consuming and has to be undertaken at relatively high levels within the organization. But the definition process is one that provides an immeasurable learning and prioritizing experience, and once the criteria are defined, they won't change very often. And within large organizations with multiple divisions, some metrics are applicable across all units, especially those tied to the overall goals and objectives of the organization.

• *We have only limited control over the results. Why should we be held accountable for things we can't control?*

While it's true that certain aspects of the public relations process are not completely controllable, much of it is manageable and, as a result, PR departments should be held accountable for delivering quality results that improve over time. As noted throughout this book, your belief that PR can't be managed almost ensures that you'll be watching from the sidelines: marginalized, minimized, and living in limbo.

• *The results will be used against us.*

Sure, some wrongheaded bosses will use the results to beat you up. But can you imagine the boss who would rather you didn't endeavor to improve or who would fault you for trying? If you're stuck in a company where your efforts to quantify and thereby improve performance get no respect, my advice is to start looking for an employer who respects you and what you do. Also keep in mind that using the results as a scorecard isn't what PR measurement is about: it's about having the feedback you need to do a better job and to *support* your efforts. What would be most harmful would be not having any results to show at all. Better to ask about ways to gain resources and recognition from your internal clients and to clearly show them the consequences of your efforts. And, yes, sometimes the results will reveal failure—but it's better to learn and improve than to ignore the results altogether. Successful organizations enjoy enormous advantages: take the necessary steps to be a member of that elite club.

 • *Management will misinterpret the results.*

Rather than providing a basis for misuse or misunderstanding, the research-based public relations process translates the insular language of public relations into the language of business, a lexicon that executives understand. And with a common vernacular, the results can be understood and validated by a much broader spectrum of marketing and communication investment decision makers.

Also keep in mind that the main purpose of the research-based public relations is to deliver the power of PR against the organization's overall goals and objectives rather than as a scorecard of individual performance. Nonetheless, when executed properly, the research-based PR process will allow for departmental and individual performance evaluations so that results at the lower levels can be aggregated to the organizational level.

 • *Management and even colleagues lack the interest and expertise to support the research we need to prove ROI.*

In the informal survey conducted at the 2004 IABC/Delahaye conference mentioned earlier, almost 85 percent of all respondents agreed with the proposition, "Lack of internal and budgetary resources is the biggest obstacle when attempting to demonstrate communications ROI." The answer to how one sells research internally can be surprisingly straightforward:

 • Advocate ROI thinking for PR within your organization.
 • Speak to internal clients once each year about the PR activities, professional attributes, and measures they value.

- Constantly and consistently communicate with internal clients to document success and demonstrate a commitment to improvement.

- Develop learning experiences to equip staff and internal clients with the insight and knowledge they need to understand what public relations ROI means.

- Set the pace in emphasizing the need for good research and evaluation and others will get the message. Having a practical expert on staff can jump-start the initiative.

- Don't perpetuate the myth that PR can't be measured. CEOs and other senior execs know better.

Turning around long-standing practices may not be quick and easy, but it can be done. IABC resources are abundant. The Institute for Public Relations offers a wide variety of free information at www.InstituteforPR.com (the source for these guidelines). Check out The Gauge, Delahaye's free subscription monthly newsletter devoted to PR research and evaluation at www.thegauge.com.

- *They will hold us to inappropriate or unfair standards.*

If the process recommended in this book is followed, you will have as much to say about the standards as anyone else (objectives-setting, remember, is a process driven by the common goal to set objectives that are reasonable, meaningful, and measurable). Having these metrics set in advance almost eliminates the risk of being unfairly or inappropriately evaluated later on, at which time there is little or nothing you can do about it.

- *This is too complicated for us.*

Some of the case studies in this book were built around complex research and evaluations, but most of them were not. Simply put, it doesn't have to be complicated. What is needed is a minimum basic set of measurements that cross various business objectives and are aligned with your objectives and strategy. The purpose of the research and evaluation, after all, is to provide clarity and understanding, not intricacy and confusion.

- *It's too expensive. We can't afford it.*

Many paths lead to the summit, but all of them begin with a single step: it would be much better to start small than to never begin. You can find many low-cost and even do-it-yourself approaches that provide insight and guidance, and it's better to be partially right than totally in the dark. And what's the cost of not making the investment? It's not just the potential for lost sales or lower market cap. In most cases the costs are much more mundane: wasted resources going toward initiatives that could easily have been avoided.

Why Wait?

At the beginning of every year, a breath of relief goes up as the past is now officially "the past," budgets are replenished, and everything again seems possible. But the recent economic climate, even if it is improved, may still bring with it a legacy of tougher times: budgets may be refreshed but they may also be smaller, and the process by which the new budget was won may have been much more rigorous than in years past.

In this environment, the question of ROI is as critical to answer as it can be difficult. But make no mistake: it is becoming more important than ever for communications professionals to *ensure*—not just measure—PR's positive return on investment. You may not be able to do anything about the past, but there's still much you can do to affect the outcome of the future. And you can begin today to ensure a positive return on your PR investment.

APPENDIXES

Appendix 1

Delahaye Executive Audit

<table>
<tr><td>

Respondent's Name:

Respondent's Phone:

Respondent's Location:

Interview Begin: _____   Interview End: _____

Length of Interview:

Interviewer's Name:

</td></tr>
</table>

Hello Mr./Ms. (**NAME ON LIST**), my name is _____, from Delahaye, an independent research firm. I have been scheduled to conduct an interview with you about WizCorp and the Wiz-Corp industry environment. Your name will remain anonymous and your responses will be strictly confidential. This interview will take about 15 minutes of your time. Is now still a good time? (**IF NOT, ARRANGE A CALLBACK TIME.**)

1. First, I'd like to list several functions within the company. While each is important, I'd like you to tell me how important you think each one is in achieving WizCorp's overall corporate goals. Please use a scale of 1 to 5 where a 5 means the function is

very important and a 1 means it is *not at all important* in achieving corporate goals. (**ROTATE ORDER. CIRCLE APPROPRIATE NUMBER BELOW. REPEAT SCALE IF NECESSARY. DO NOT READ "DON'T KNOW."**)

How important is . . .

	Very Important				Not at All Important	Don't Know
Customer service	5	4	3	2	1	9
Sales	5	4	3	2	1	9
Marketing/Advertising	5	4	3	2	1	9
Training	5	4	3	2	1	9
Public/Media relations	5	4	3	2	1	9
Human resources	5	4	3	2	1	9
Government and regulatory affairs	5	4	3	2	1	9
Finance	5	4	3	2	1	9
Legal	5	4	3	2	1	9

2. Now I'd like to list some activities that might be used to measure the effectiveness of the media relations function within any company among your competitors. And by "media relations," we mean the department that deals with the print, broadcast, and Internet news media rather than advertising or media buying. I'd like you to tell me how important you think each of these activities is in measuring the effectiveness of media relations, again using a scale of 1 to 5 where a 5 means it is *very important* and a 1 means it is *not at all important*. (**ROTATE ORDER. CIRCLE APPRO-PRIATE NUMBER BELOW. REPEAT SCALE IF NECES-SARY. DO NOT READ "DON'T KNOW."**)

How important is it for a media relations function to . . .

	Very Important				Not at All Important	Don't Know
Increase awareness of the company	5	4	3	2	1	9
Increase awareness of the company's products	5	4	3	2	1	9
Change attitudes about the company	5	4	3	2	1	9
Deliver key messages	5	4	3	2	1	9
Enhance the company's image or reputation	5	4	3	2	1	9
Obtain favorable or balanced media treatment	5	4	3	2	1	9
Prevent problems	5	4	3	2	1	9
Solve problems	5	4	3	2	1	9
Increase sales leads	5	4	3	2	1	9
Increase sales	5	4	3	2	1	9
Generate a high volume of media clippings	5	4	3	2	1	9

3. Now I'm going to read for you these same activities and ask you to tell me how well you think WizCorp's Corporate Media Relations function does on each of them compared to competitors.

Do you think WizCorp's Corporate Media Relations function is better than, just as good, almost as good, worse than, or much worse than competitors are on . . . (**ROTATE ORDER. CIRCLE APPROPRIATE NUMBER BELOW. REPEAT RESPONSE ALTERNATIVES IF NECESSARY. DO NOT READ "DON'T KNOW."**)

	Better	Just as Good	Almost as Good	Worse	Much Worse	Don't Know
Increasing awareness of the company	5	4	3	2	1	9
Increasing awareness of the company's products	5	4	3	2	1	9
Changing attitudes about the company	5	4	3	2	1	9
Delivering key messages	5	4	3	2	1	9
Enhancing the company's image	5	4	3	2	1	9
Obtaining favorable media treatment	5	4	3	2	1	9
Preventing problems	5	4	3	2	1	9
Solving problems	5	4	3	2	1	9
Increasing sales leads	5	4	3	2	1	9
Increasing sales	5	4	3	2	1	9
Generating a high volume of media clippings	5	4	3	2	1	9

4. I'm going to list for you some professional skills and abilities that media relations professionals within any company might be expected to have. I would like you to tell me how important you think it is that media relations professionals have each of these skills using a scale of 1 to 5 where a 5 means it is *very important* and a 1 means it is *not at all important*. (ROTATE ORDER. CIRCLE APPROPRIATE NUMBER BELOW. REPEAT SCALE IF NECESSARY. DO NOT READ "DON'T KNOW.")

How would you rate the importance of media relations professionals having . . .

	Very Important				Not at All Important	Don't Know
Friendly relations with media contacts	5	4	3	2	1	9
A measurable results orientation	5	4	3	2	1	9
The ability to work effectively with the media	5	4	3	2	1	9
Problem-solving skills	5	4	3	2	1	9
General business knowledge	5	4	3	2	1	9
Written and oral advocacy skills on company issues	5	4	3	2	1	9
The ability to represent the company in public situations	5	4	3	2	1	9
Presentation skills	5	4	3	2	1	9
Writing skills	5	4	3	2	1	9
Knowledge of the industry	5	4	3	2	1	9
Interpersonal skills	5	4	3	2	1	9

5. Now I'm going to read to you these same skills and abilities and ask you to tell me how strong you think WizCorp's Corporate Media Relations function is on each of them using a scale of 1 to 5 where a 5 means they are *very strong* and a 1 means they are *not at all strong*. (ROTATE ORDER. CIRCLE APPROPRIATE NUMBER BELOW. REPEAT SCALE IF NECESSARY. DO NOT READ "DON'T KNOW.")

How strong would you say WizCorp's Media Relations professionals are on . . .

	Very Strong				Not at All Strong	Don't Know
Friendly relations with media contacts	5	4	3	2	1	9
A measurable results orientation	5	4	3	2	1	9
The ability to work effectively with the media	5	4	3	2	1	9
Problem-solving skills	5	4	3	2	1	9
General business knowledge	5	4	3	2	1	9
Written and oral advocacy skills on company issues	5	4	3	2	1	9
The ability to represent the company in public situations	5	4	3	2	1	9
Presentation skills	5	4	3	2	1	9
Writing skills	5	4	3	2	1	9
Knowledge of the industry	5	4	3	2	1	9
Interpersonal skills	5	4	3	2	1	9

6. I'm going to read for you some services provided by a media relations department that might be valued within a company. I would like you to tell me how valuable you think each of these services are in helping to achieve company goals using a scale of 1 to 5, where a 5 means it is *very valuable* and a 1 means it is *not at all valuable*. (ROTATE ORDER. CIRCLE APPROPRIATE NUMBER BELOW. REPEAT SCALE IF NECESSARY. DO NOT READ "DON'T KNOW.")

How valuable would you say is . . .

	Very Valuable				Not at All Valuable	Don't Know
Keeping management apprised of stakeholder opinions and concerns	5	4	3	2	1	9
Building support for company positions from key stakeholders	5	4	3	2	1	9
Attracting potential customers to existing sales channels	5	4	3	2	1	9
Cultivating a customer base that is predisposed to buy from WizCorp	5	4	3	2	1	9
Informing customers of company changes that will affect them	5	4	3	2	1	9
Responding to media questions in an open, honest, and timely manner	5	4	3	2	1	9
Promoting communications support (like speech writing, project planning, or event coordination)	5	4	3	2	1	9
Identifying potential roadblocks to consumer acceptance of company plans, products, and actions	5	4	3	2	1	9

	Very Valuable				Not at All Valuable	Don't Know
Providing counsel to management on dealing with news media	5	4	3	2	1	9
Seeking news coverage of company products and innovations	5	4	3	2	1	9
Counseling management on communications with key stakeholders	5	4	3	2	1	9
Providing stakeholder research for company and departmental planning	5	4	3	2	1	9

7. Now, I'll read a list of these same services and ask you to tell me how well you think WizCorp's Corporate Media Relations function does in providing each of them using a scale of 1 to 5 where a 5 means they do an excellent job and a 1 means they do a poor job. **(ROTATE ORDER. CIRCLE APPROPRIATE NUMBER BELOW. REPEAT SCALE IF NECESSARY. DO NOT READ "DON'T KNOW.")**

How good of a job would you say WizCorp's Corporate Media Relations does on . . .

	Excellent Job				Poor Job	Don't Know
Keeping management apprised of stakeholder opinions and concerns	5	4	3	2	1	9

	Excellent Job				Poor Job	Don't Know
Building support for company positions from key stakeholders	5	4	3	2	1	9
Attracting potential customers to existing sales channels	5	4	3	2	1	9
Cultivating a customer base that is predisposed to buy from WizCorp	5	4	3	2	1	9
Informing customers of company changes that will affect them	5	4	3	2	1	9
Responding to media questions in an open, honest, and timely manner	5	4	3	2	1	9
Promoting communications support (like speech writing, project planning, or event coordination)	5	4	3	2	1	9
Identifying potential roadblocks to consumer acceptance of company plans, products, and actions	5	4	3	2	1	9
Providing counsel to management on dealing with news media	5	4	3	2	1	9
Seeking news coverage of company products and innovations	5	4	3	2	1	9

	Excellent Job				Poor Job	Don't Know
Counseling management on communications with key stakeholders	5	4	3	2	1	9
Providing stakeholder research for company and departmental planning	5	4	3	2	1	9

8. There are several key messages that WizCorp Corporate Media Relations delivers to the media. I'd like to read each of these messages to you and ask you to tell me how successfully you think each of them are currently being communicated using a scale of 1 to 5 where a 5 means *very successful* and a 1 means *not at all successful*. (**ROTATE ORDER. CIRCLE APPROPRIATE NUMBER BELOW. REPEAT SCALE IF NECESSARY. DO NOT READ "DON'T KNOW."**)

How successfully would you say this message is being communicated:

	Very Successful				Not at All Successful	Don't Know
WizCorp products are of the highest quality	5	4	3	2	1	9
WizCorp is *number one in the world*	5	4	3	2	1	9
WizCorp helps consumers see, look, and feel better through *innovative* technology and design	5	4	3	2	1	9

	Very Successful				Not at All Successful	Don't Know
WizCorp is the *global* leader	5	4	3	2	1	9
WizCorp has a new top management team; its troubles of the past are ancient history and no longer impact nor reflect the way the company does business	5	4	3	2	1	9
WizCorp has a bright future	5	4	3	2	1	9
WizCorp is a good investment	5	4	3	2	1	9
WizCorp is a good place to work	5	4	3	2	1	9

9. I would now like to change the topic and ask you about "Integrated Marketing Communications." Integrated Marketing Communications is an approach to coordinating advertising, direct marketing, sales promotion, and media relations. By managing your communications efforts as a whole, the theory is, you will be better able to plan a cohesive, integrated message strategy that can be tracked and evaluated over time and that will maximize your communications impact.

Please tell me the extent to which you think Integrated Marketing Communications is practiced at WizCorp using a scale of 1 to 5 where a 5 means it is *practiced completely* and a 1 means it is *not practiced at all*. (**ROTATE ORDER. CIRCLE APPROPRIATE NUMBER BELOW. REPEAT SCALE IF NECESSARY. DO NOT READ "DON'T KNOW."**)

	Practiced Completely				Not Practiced at All	Don't Know
Place of "Integrated Marketing Communications"	5	4	3	2	1	9

10. There are a number of media sources that our company could use to tell its story. I'd like to list these media and ask you to tell me how "impactful" (credible, involving) you think each of these media sources are in reaching WizCorp's target audiences, using a scale of 1 to 5 where a 5 means *most impactful* and a 1 means *least impactful*. (**ROTATE ORDER. IF NECESSARY, READ EXAMPLES OF EACH MEDIA TYPE. CIRCLE APPROPRIATE NUMBER BELOW. REPEAT SCALE IF NECESSARY. DO NOT READ "DON'T KNOW."**)

How impactful would you say is/are . . .

	Most Impactful				Least Impactful	Don't Know
General interest magazines (*People*)	5	4	3	2	1	9
News magazines (*Time, Newsweek*)	5	4	3	2	1	9
Business magazines (*Fortune, Forbes*)	5	4	3	2	1	9
Trade journals	5	4	3	2	1	9
Local daily newspapers (*The Democrat & Chronicle*)	5	4	3	2	1	9
Local weekly newspapers (*Palmyra Courier Journal*)	5	4	3	2	1	9
National newspapers (*USA Today, NY Times*)	5	4	3	2	1	9

	Most Impactful				Least Impactful	Don't Know
Business newspapers (*Wall Street Journal*)	5	4	3	2	1	9
Local television	5	4	3	2	1	9
Network television (CBS, ABC)	5	4	3	2	1	9
Cable television (CNBC, MSNBC)	5	4	3	2	1	9
Radio (ABC Radio)	5	4	3	2	1	9
Internet news (Yahoo!)	5	4	3	2	1	9
Wire services (AP, Bloomberg)	5	4	3	2	1	9

11A. In your opinion, which Eye-care company has the best media relations department? (**DO NOT READ LIST. CIRCLE ONLY ONE NUMBER BELOW.**)

WizCorp	1
OptiCorp	2
FineCorp	3
BestBiz	4
ColossaCorp	5
FriendlyCorp	6
Other (specify) _____	7
(**DO NOT READ**) Don't know	9

11B. What does this company do that makes it the best?

_____

_____

_____

12A. When the choices extend to *all* companies, including competitive companies and beyond, which company, in your opinion, has the best media relations department?

WizCorp   1

Other (specify) _____   2

(DO NOT READ)   Don't know   9

12B. **(IF DIFFERENT FROM 11A)** What does this company do to make it the best?

_____

_____

_____

THANK RESPONDENT AND END INTERVIEW.

Appendix 2

Delahaye Media Demographic Audit

For: JAGUAR
Presented By: Delahaye Public Relations Research
February, 1998

Introduction

- The Delahaye Media Demographic Audit is a public relations tool based on in-depth audience profiles of print and broadcast national and local consumer media.

- Over 700 criteria are accessible through the Delahaye Media Demographic Audit, including demographics (age, gender, marital status, etc.), psychographics ("Aging Yuppie," "Conservative Empty Nester," etc.), leisure activities and lifestyles, as well as ownership, intent to buy, and usage/consumption patterns for over 100 brand names.

- The resulting in-depth profiles are matched to the media these audiences read, watch, and listen to.

- The Delahaye Media Demographic Audit is used to create more targeted media plans and more strategic public relations programs in order to reach and speak meaningfully to one's target audience.

Use the Audit to:

- Identify key markets.
- Create more focused media plans.

- Produce and distribute more targeted and localized release materials. "Pitch" the media *scientifically*.

- Evaluate programs based on *Target Audience Reached* as well as general Circulation or Audience.

- Better integrate public relations strategies with other tools within the marketing and communications mix.

- The Delahaye Media Demographic Audit is available exclusively through Delahaye Public Relations Research.

Methodology

- The Delahaye Media Demographic Audit is based on a proprietary integration and application of Simmons' and International Demographics' demographic databases.

- The data contained within the Delahaye Media Demographic Audit is the result of in-depth interviews with statistically representative and projectable population samples.

- Delahaye analysts identify which of over 700 criteria best match the client's target audience and apply these criteria through a database search.

- The resulting report can be used to identify the markets with the highest number or highest concentration of the target population. Further, it can identify which media *within* and *from outside* these markets will reach the highest number or highest concentration of the target population.

- The Delahaye Media Demographic Audit data was analyzed and formatted to create this report.

Note to the Reader: The data contained in this report is based on relatively small sample sizes. As such, it should be viewed as directional rather than statistically significant.

Background

- Jaguar requested Delahaye's Media Demographic Audit in order to identify which consumer media—print and broadcast, national and local—had the highest degrees of penetration and reach within their top 15 markets.

- Delahaye identified those media in the top 15 markets with the highest concentration of (1) people earning more than $100,000 annually who (2) intend to buy a new car within the next 12 months and (3) who plan to spend more than $20,000 on their new car.

- The resulting analysis will be used in an effort to more effectively target Jaguar's target audience through the media they read, watch, and listen to.

The results will also help Jaguar to achieve more fully integrated marketing solutions with advertising and direct-mail promotions:

- Supplementing Jaguar's advertising buys within the top 15 markets by targeting PR to the media in which Jaguar *doesn't* advertise.

- By providing Jaguar with a number of media options within each market—many of which are counterintuitive choices.

- To apply in creating and implementing the localized press release program in 1998.

Executive Summary

- Within the top 15 markets, Jaguar has a broad base of media opportunities: In each market, advertising is targeting only one newspaper per market. In New York, for example, there are over 30 *additional* outlets to pursue—print and broadcast.

- Many media outlets are "counterintuitive" choices—weekly newspapers, independent TV stations, for example, even free shoppers.

- In addition to the major "daily newspaper of record," top spots are occupied by local general interest magazines—*New York Magazine* and *Los Angeles Magazine*. Local sports channels, evening TV news programs, and business weeklies also ranked among the best media types. On the other hand, radio did not register—which is not to say that radio shouldn't be included in the company's media plan, only that this result should be factored into the strategy.

- Within the strict definition of this search, Atlanta, Miami, and San Francisco represent the highest *percentage of total population* matching the Jaguar target (Philadelphia and Phoenix the lowest). The average was about 2.5 percent of the general population.

- In terms of the *number* of target customers, New York, San Francisco, and Chicago are on top. San Francisco is the only city to appear on both lists. (Phoenix and Boston have the lowest populations.)

The Media Audit: Atlanta

Population: 394,017
Jaguar Target Population: 44,000

Media	Reach (000's)	Reach (percent)
ATL-Fox Sportsouth	43	96.8
ATL-Jrnl/Const Sdy	42	94.12
ATL-Jrnl/Const Dly	40	89.44
ATL-Creative Loafing	34	76.64
ATL-Neighbor Newspp	34	76.23
ATL-Journal Dly	28	63.14

Media	Reach (000's)	Reach (percent)
ATL-Southern Living	27	60.15
ATL-Constitution Dly	26	58.04
ATL-WSB-TV M-F LNEE	21	47
ATL-WSB-TV M-F LNLE	20	45.43
ATL-Atlanta Magazine	19	43.47
ATL-Georgia Trend	16	34.84
ATL-Business Chron	14	31.93
ATL-Sports&Fitness	8	18.23
ATL-WSB-TV M-F LNEM	8	17.84
ATL-WXIA-TV M-F LNEE	7	16.09
ATL-Jewish Times	3	7.36
ATL-WXIA-TV M-F LNEM	2	4.35

The Media Audit: Boston

Population: 574,283
Jaguar Target population: 16,000

Media	Reach (000's)	Reach (percent)
BOS-Boston Globe Sdy	16	100
BOS-Boston Globe Dly	13	79.26
BOS-WCVB-TV M-F LNLE	12	73.45
BOS-Boston Herald Sunday	11	66.07
BOS-Boston Herald Dly	9	56.63
BOS-WCVB-TV M-F LNEE	9	53.67
BOS-Qncy Pat Ledger Dly	8	49.99
BOS-WBZ-TV M-F LNEM	8	49.95
BOS-New England Cable News	8	49.17
BOS-WBZ-TV M-F LNLE	7	43.71

Media	Reach (000's)	Reach (percent)
BOS-Improper Bostonian	6	40.03
BOS-WBZ-TV M-F LNEE	6	38.61
BOS-Yankee	5	31.39
BOS-Boston Magazine	4	23.92
BOS-Law Eagle-Tribune Dly	3	20.69
BOS-Boston Parent	2	13.22
BOS-Business Journal	2	13.22
BOS-The Tab	2	13.22
BOS-WLVI-TV M-F LNPT	2	10.69

The Media Audit: Chicago

Population: 2,783,726
Jaguar Target Population: 54,000

Media	Reach (000's)	Reach (percent)
CHI-Crain's Chi Bus	48	87.75
CHI-Sports Channel	48	87.14
CHI-Tribune Sdy	46	84.35
CHI-Tribune Dly	44	80.23
CHI-Chicagoland TV News	42	76.35
CHI-WLS-TV M-F LNLE	39	71.32
CHI-Sun-Times Sdy	38	70.16
CHI-WBBM-TV M-F LNLE	32	59.07
CHI-Sun-Times Dly	31	57.19
CHI-WMAQ-TV M-F LNEE	29	53.81
CHI-Chicago Magazine	27	48.73
CHI-WGN-TV M-F LNPT	24	43.51

Media	Reach (000's)	Reach (percent)
CHI-WMAQ-TV M-F LNLE	24	43.47
CHI-WMAQ-TV M-F LNEM	20	36.4
CHI-FX	20	36.12
CHI-WLS-TV M-F LNEM	18	32.47
CHI-WLS-TV M-F LNEE	15	28.36
CHI-North Shore Mag.	12	22.85
CHI-Chicago Reader	10	18.29
CHI-New City	10	17.87
CHI-Windy City Times	6	10.56
CHI-WFLD-TV M-F LNEM	6	10.56
CHI-Chi Social Magazine	6	10.32
CHI-WBBM-TV M-F LNEM	3	5.73

The Media Audit: Detroit

Population: 1,027,974
Jaguar Target Population: 28,000

Media	Reach (000's)	Reach (percent)
DET-News/Free Press Sunday	25	86.07
DET-Free Press/News Dly	25	86.01
DET-Home & Garden-HGTV	21	71.35
DET-Free Press Dly	18	61.13
DET-Detroit News Dly	15	53.66
DET-WXYZ-TV M-F LNLE	15	52.09
DET-Crain's Det Bus	13	46.04
DET-Corporate Det	12	42.5
DET-WXYZ-TV M-F LNEE	8	29.35
DET-Oakland Press Sunday	8	26.06

Media	Reach (000's)	Reach (percent)
DET-Oakland Press Dly	8	26.06
DET-WDIV-TV M-F LNEM	7	22.58
DET-WKBD-TV M-F LNPT	6	19.13
DET-The Mirror	4	14.04
DET-WDIV-TV M-F LNEE	4	14.04
DET-Det Jewish News	3	12.13
DET-WXYZ-TV M-F LNEM	2	7.34

The Media Audit: Houston

Population: 1,630,553
Jaguar Target Population: 43,000

Media	Reach (000's)	Reach (percent)
HOU-KTRK-TV M-F LNEE	40	93.38
HOU-Chronicle Dly	40	93.08
HOU-KTRK-TV M-F LNLE	37	85.96
HOU-KHOU-TV M-F LNEE	36	84.38
HOU-Chronicle Sdy	35	82.11
HOU-KPRC-TV M-F LNEM	35	81.34
HOU-KPRC-TV M-F LNLE	18	41.17
HOU-KPRC-TV M-F LNEE	17	38.76
HOU-Texas Monthly	15	34.81
HOU-Houston Press	14	32.62
HOU-Business Journal	7	15.87
HOU-Fox Sports Swest	6	13.37
HOU-Greensheet	5	11.22
HOU-KRIV-TV M-F LNPT	4	8.83

Media	Reach (000's)	Reach (percent)
HOU-Texas Business	2	5.42
HOU-KRIV-TV M-F LNEM	1	3.18
HOU-Brazospt Fcts Dly	1	3.18
HOU-Brazospt Fcts Sunday	1	3.18

The Media Audit: Los Angeles

Population: 2,967,000
Jaguar Target Population: 51,000

Media	Reach (000's)	Reach (percent)
LA-Business Journal	51	100
LA-Pennysaver	43	83
LA-Los Angeles Magazine	43	83
LA-KNBC-TV M-F LNEE	32	62
LA-L.A. Weekly	31	60
LA-KNBC-TV M-F LNLE	28	55
LA-Times Daily	28	54
LA-Times Sdy	28	54
LA-KNBC-TV M-F LNEM	22	42
LA-KTLA-TV M-F LNPT	15	29
LA-KCBS-TV M-F LNEE	8	16
LA-KTLA-TV M-F LNEM	4	9
LA-New Times LA	4	9
LA-Orange Co News TV	3	6
LA-Orange Co Reg Dly	3	6
LA-Orange Co Reg Sdy	3	6
LA-La Opinion Para Ti	2	5

The Media Audit: Miami

Population: 349,000
Jaguar Target Population: 18,000

Media	Reach (000's)	Reach (percent)
MFL-Ft L Sun-Sent Sunday	13	71
MFL-Ft L Sun-Sent Dly	12	66
MFL-WSVN-TV M-F LNPT	9	46
MFL-Sunshine Network	8	42
MFL-WPLG-TV M-F LNEE	7	37
MFL-WSVN-TV M-F LNEM	6	33
MFL-Miami Herald Dly	5	29
MFL-Florida Trend	5	26
MFL-The Flyer	4	23
MFL-WSVN-TV M-F LNLE	4	20
MFL-WPLG-TV M-F LNLE	4	20
MFL-Miami Herald Sdy	3	17
MFL-South Florida Mg	2	13
MFL-WPLG-TV M-F LNEM	2	12
MFL-WTVJ-TV M-F LNEM	2	9
MFL-Pennysaver	2	9
MFL-WTVJ-TV M-F LNEE	1	8
MFL-WTVJ-TV M-F LNLE	1	8
MFL-Ocean Drive Magazine	0	1
MFL-New Times	0	1
MFL-Fashion Spectrum	0	1
MFL-X S	0	1

The Media Audit: New York

Population: 7,322,564
Jaguar Target Population: 161,000

Media	Reach (000's)	Reach (percent)
NY-New York Magazine	145	90
NY-The New Yorker	119	73
NY-Madison Sq Garden	111	69
NY-Shoppers Guide	106	65
NY-WABC-TV M-F LNLE	99	61
NY-New York Post Dly	81	50
NY-WNBC-TV M-F LNLE	78	48
NY-Entertainment TV	75	46
NY-Long Isl News 12	70	43
NY-New York Times Sunday	65	40
NY-Newark Star-Ledger-Sunday	64	40
NY-Daily News Dly	62	39
NY-Pennysaver	60	37
NY-WABC-TV M-F LNEE	57	35
NY-WABC-TV M-F LNEM	57	35
NY-Newark Star-Ledger Dly	53	33
NY-WNBC-TV M-F LNEE	53	33
NY-Daily News Sdy	39	24
NY-WPIX-TV M-F LNPT	39	24
NY-Newsday Daily	35	22
NY-Sportschannel	35	22
NY-Crain's NY Bus	31	19
NY-New York Post Sdy	27	17

Media	Reach (000's)	Reach (percent)
NY-Asbury Pk Press Dly	23	14
NY-Newsy Sunday	19	12
NY-Village Voice	17	10
NY-WNYW-TV M-F LNPT	17	10
NY-Jersey Journal-Dly	15	10
NY-WRNN-TV Newschannel	15	10
NY-The Marketer	13	8
NY-WCBS-TV M-F LNLE	12	8
NY-WWOR-TV M-F LNPT	11	7
NY-New York 1	9	6
NY-Amsterdam News	7	5
NY-Asbury Pk Press Sdy	7	5

The Media Audit: Philadelphia

Population: 1,585,577
Jaguar Target Population: 17,000

Media	Reach (000's)	Reach (percent)
PHIL-Inquirer Sdy	14	80.13
PHIL-Philadelphia Mg	10	56.39
PHIL-Inquirer Dly	7	40.83
PHIL-News/Inquirer Dly	7	40.25
PHIL-Dly Local News Dly	4	25.03
PHIL-S Philadelphia Review	4	23.66
PHIL-Cam Courier-Post Sunday	4	23.66
PHIL-Main Line Times	3	16.52

Media	Reach (000's)	Reach (percent)
PHIL-Dly Local News Sunday	3	15.7
PHIL-Shoppers Guide	2	9.32
PHIL-Philadelphia Weekly	0	2.15
PHIL-Bucks City Midweek	0	0.5
PHIL-Daily News Dly	0	0.5

The Media Audit: Phoenix

Population: 983,403
Jaguar Target Population: 8,000

Media	Reach (000's)	Reach (percent)
PHO-Home & Garden	7	88.05
PHO-Ariz Republic Dly	7	80.69
PHO-Ariz Republic Sunday	7	80.69
PHO-Today Arizona Woman	7	80
PHO-KTVK-TV M-F LNEE	6	74.02
PHO-New Times	5	57.65
PHO-Phoenix Magazine	5	56.6
PHO-KPNX-TV M-F LNEE	3	38.35
PHO-Scottsdale Scene	2	20.09
PHO-Independent News	2	20.09
PHO-KPNX-TV M-F LNLE	2	20.09
PHO-KPHO-TV M-F LNLE	2	19.31
PHO-KTVK-TV M-F LNEM	2	18.25
PHO-KTVK-TV M-F LNLE	2	18.25
PHO-KNXV-TV M-F LNLE	2	18.25

The Media Audit: San Francisco

Population: 723,959
Jaguar Target Population: 60,000

Media	Reach (000's)	Reach (percent)
SF-SF Chronicle Dly	57	93.96
SF-Potpourri	52	85.95
SF-SF Examiner/Chronicle Sdy	48	78.99
SF-SJ Mercury News Dly	47	77.21
SF-Metro	32	53.06
SF-SJ Mercury News Sunday	28	46.32
SF-SF Examiner Dly	19	32.3
SF-SF Focus	17	28.71
SF-SF Independent	16	26.18
SF-SF Bay Guardian	15	25.43
SF-SF Weekly	13	21.05
SF-Daily Review Dly	9	15.07
SF-Daily Review Sdy	9	15.07

Appendix 3

Delahaye Journalist Audit

Respondent's Name:

Respondent's Phone:

Publication:

Respondent's Address:

Interview Begin: _____   Interview End: _____

Length of Interview:

Interviewer's Name:

ASK FOR NAME ON LIST. IF PERSON IS NOT AVAILABLE, CONFIRM THAT THIS PERSON IS STILL THE PRIMARY REPORTER OR EDITOR OF *TECHNOLOGY TOPICS*. IF NOT, ASK FOR THE NEW PERSON. IF NO NAME IS ON THE LIST, ASK FOR THE PERSON WHO IS THE PRIMARY REPORTER OR EDITOR OF *TECHNOLOGY*.

Hello Mr./Ms. (**NAME ON LIST**), my name is _____, from Delahaye, an independent research firm. We're conducting a brief survey among media representatives for the Technology industry. You have been randomly selected from a list of journalists working throughout the country. Your name will remain anonymous and your responses will be strictly confidential. Do you have about 10 minutes to answer some questions? (**IF NOT, ARRANGE A CALLBACK TIME.**)

1. I'm going to read some attributes that might apply to any technology company's public relations activity. For each attribute, please tell me how much you value this particular attribute using a scale of 1 to 5 where 5 means it is *very valuable* and 1 means it is *not at all valuable*. (**ROTATE ORDER. CIRCLE APPROPRIATE NUMBER BELOW. REPEAT SCALE IF NECESSARY. DO NOT READ "DON'T KNOW."**)

In doing your job, how valuable would you say is/are . . .

	Very Valuable				Not at All Valuable	Don't Know
Having friendly relations with public relations people	5	4	3	2	1	9
Public relations people who are easy to get in touch with	5	4	3	2	1	9
Public relations people responding quickly to inquiries	5	4	3	2	1	9
Knowing who to call on a specific issue	5	4	3	2	1	9
Receiving regular PR calls from them	5	4	3	2	1	9
Press materials that are well written	5	4	3	2	1	9
Press materials that are newsworthy	5	4	3	2	1	9

	Very Valuable				Not at All Valuable	Don't Know
Having access to top management	5	4	3	2	1	9
PR people calling with newsworthy pitches	5	4	3	2	1	9
Press conferences that are worth attending	5	4	3	2	1	9
PR people giving you exclusives	5	4	3	2	1	9

2. Now I'm going to read you these same attributes and ask you to apply them to several technology companies' PR departments. For each company, please tell me how much you agree or disagree with the statement using a scale of 1 to 5 where 5 means you *strongly agree* and 1 means you *strongly disagree*. (**READ STATEMENTS ONE AT A TIME AND OBTAIN RATING FOR EACH COMPANY BEFORE MOVING ON TO THE NEXT STATEMENT. ROTATE ORDER OF STATEMENTS. ENTER ONE NUMBER FROM 1 TO 5 IN THE APPROPRIATE SPACE BELOW. ENTER A "9" FOR "DON'T KNOW." REPEAT SCALE IF NECESSARY.**)

How much would you agree that . . .

	WizCom	*OptiCom*	*Competitor 2*	*Competitor 3*	*Competitor 4*
You have friendly relations with (**COMPANY'S**) public relations people	____	____	____	____	____
(**COMPANY'S**) PR people are easy to get in touch with	____	____	____	____	____

	WizCom	OptiCom	Competitor 2	Competitor 3	Competitor 4
(COMPANY'S) public relations people respond quickly to inquiries	___	___	___	___	___
At **(COMPANY)** you know who to call on a specific issue	___	___	___	___	___
You receive regular PR calls from **(COMPANY)**	___	___	___	___	___
You receive press materials from **(COMPANY)** that are well written	___	___	___	___	___
You receive press materials from **(COMPANY)** that are newsworthy	___	___	___	___	___
You have access to **(COMPANY'S)** top management	___	___	___	___	___
(COMPANY'S) PR people call with newsworthy pitches	___	___	___	___	___

	WizCom	OptiCom	Competitor 2	Competitor 3	Competitor 4
(COMPANY) holds press conferences that are worth attending	_____	_____	_____	_____	_____
(COMPANY'S) PR people give you exclusives	_____	_____	_____	_____	_____

3. What is your most preferred method for receiving press materials? **(DO NOT READ LIST. ACCEPT ONLY ONE AN-SWER. CIRCLE THE APPROPRIATE NUMBER BELOW.)**

Fax	0
Mail	1
E-mail	2
PR newswire	3
Businesswire	4
Telephone call	5
Teleconferences	6
Videoconferences	7
Other (specify)	8
Don't know	99

4A. Who within a technology company would you prefer to contact first, someone from corporate headquarters or someone from a local office?

Corporate headquarters	1
Local office	2
No difference/preference	3
Don't know	99

4B. Who would you most prefer to contact first at a company's **(READ RESPONSE FROM Q4A IF "CORPORATE HEAD-QUARTERS" OR "LOCAL OFFICE")? (READ LIST. AC-CEPT ONLY ONE ANSWER. CIRCLE THE APPROPRIATE NUMBER BELOW.)**

A company-designated media contact	1
Any PR person who is available	2
A relevant marketing or product person	3
Personal contacts within the company but outside the formal channels	4
(DO NOT READ) Other (specify) _____	5
(DO NOT READ) Don't know	99

4C. I'd like to read these sources within a company's **(READ RESPONSE FROM Q4A IF "CORPORATE HEADQUAR-TERS" OR "LOCAL OFFICE")** again and ask you to tell me how credible you think each of them is using a scale from 1 to 5 where 5 means *most credible* and 1 is *least credible*. **(ROTATE ORDER. CIR-CLE APPROPRIATE NUMBER BELOW. REPEAT SCALE IF NECESSARY. DO NOT READ "DON'T KNOW.")**

How credible would you say is/are . . .

	Most Credible				Least Credible	Don't Know
A company-designated media contact	5	4	3	2	1	9
Any PR person who is available	5	4	3	2	1	9
A relevant marketing or product person	5	4	3	2	1	9
Personal contacts within the company but outside formal channels	5	4	3	2	1	9

5A. And when you're working on an important technology story with a tight deadline, which company would you be most likely to contact first? (**DO NOT READ LIST. ACCEPT ONLY ONE ANSWER. CIRCLE THE APPROPRIATE NUMBER BELOW.**)

WizCom	1
OptiCom	2
Competitor 2	3
Competitor 3	4
Competitor 4	5
(**DO NOT READ**) Other (specify) _____	6
(**DO NOT READ**) Don't know	99
(**DO NOT READ**) Never call a company	0

5B. Why do you call this company? (**WRITE DOWN RESPONSE.**)

6A. Overall, which technology company has the best public relations department? (**DO NOT READ LIST. CIRCLE ONLY ONE NUMBER BELOW.**)

WizCom	1
OptiCom	2
Competitor 2	3
Competitor 3	4
Competitor 4	5
Other (specify) _____	6
Don't know	99

6B. What does this company do that makes it the best? (**WRITE DOWN RESPONSE.**)

THANK RESPONDENT AND END INTERVIEW.

Index

About the International Association
of Business Communicators

The International Association of Business Communicators (IABC) is a global network of over thirteen thousand communication professionals in sixty-seven countries, one hundred chapters, and ten thousand organizations. Established in 1970, IABC ensures that its members have the skills and resources to progress in their careers, develop and share best practices, set standards of excellence, build credibility and respect for the profession, and unite as a community. IABC members practice the disciplines of corporate communication, public relations, employee communication, marketing communication, media relations, community relations, public affairs, investor relations, and government relations.

Programs

IABC sponsors several conferences throughout the year in addition to its annual international conference. To further the education of communication professionals, IABC offers monthly teleseminars and Web seminars. IABC honors the best in the profession with the Gold Quill Awards program and the accreditation program. IABC also maintains an online job board.

Publications

The publishing division of IABC offers books, manuals, and communication templates on a number of organizational communication topics. IABC also publishes the award-winning, bimonthly magazine, *Communication World*, and a monthly online newsletter, *CW Bulletin*.

Research

The IABC Research Foundation is a nonprofit corporation dedicated to the support and advancement of organizational communication by delivering research findings vital to the profession. The Foundation translates leading-edge communication theory into real-world practice, helping communicators be effective and visionary in their work. Founded in 1970, the Foundation is building a research portfolio aligned with a new research agenda. The Foundation offers grants for communication research in support of this agenda. Learn more about the International Association of Business Communicators at www.iabc.com.